Written on the Heart

Studies in the
Gospel of Matthew

Eugene A. Smith

Written on the Heart

Freedom Alive Ministries
www.freedomalive.ca

ISBN: 1-931178-87-9

All scripture quotations are taken from the
New King James Version
(all bold face throughout text added by the author)

Published by:

Vision Publishing
940 Montecito Way
Ramona, CA 92065

www.vision.edu

This book is dedicated to my two sons,
Jeremy and Jesse,
who have shared their dad with the world.

Contents

Section V.

Waiting for the End

Section VI.

The Beatitudes

Section I.

Matthew, His Readers, Purpose and Arrangement

Section I

Chapter One

A terrible time of calamity is about to fall upon the nation of Israel. Matthew writes to prepare fellow believers in Christ for the prospect of a final and total break with the faith they had been taught since their childhood days.

The Times and World of Matthew

Who is the Author?

The author of each New Testament gospel does not identify himself directly. Therefore, Biblical scholars search the text for convincing clues to determine the authorship of each gospel. That Matthew wrote this book has not been disputed seriously. In addition, early church tradition supports this conclusion.

Matthew was one of the twelve disciples of Christ; therefore, he was an eyewitness to many of the events recorded. His own conversion is described in the scripture quoted below:

*"As Jesus passed on from there, He saw a man named Matthew sitting at the tax office. **And He said to him, 'Follow Me.' So he arose and followed Him.** Now it happened, as Jesus sat at the table in the house, that behold, many tax collectors and sinners came and sat down with Him and His disciples. And when the Pharisees saw it, they said to His disciples, 'Why does your Teacher eat with tax collectors and sinners?' When Jesus heard that, He said to them, 'Those who are well have no need of a*

physician, but those who are sick. But go and learn what this means: 'I desire mercy and not sacrifice.' For I did not come to call the righteous, but sinners, to repentance. " (Matt. 9:9-13)

Prior to following Christ, Matthew was a tax collector; consequently, the public despised him. No doubt his inclusion among the other disciples caused considerable concern for the disciples and the general population of Israel.

It is interesting to note that this gospel, written by a former tax collector, often uses monetary terms not found elsewhere in scripture. Only Matthew's gospel refers to "talents" (Matt. 25:14-30), the "stater" (a piece of money – Matt. 17:27), and the "drachma" (tribute or double drachma – Matt. 17:24). Only in this gospel is the story of Jesus paying the temple tax recorded (Matt: 17:24-27). Also, this is the only gospel that records the amount, thirty pieces of silver, for which Jesus was betrayed (Matt. 26:15).

Some of the parables found in Matthew's gospel use money as a teaching tool: the story of a treasure hidden in a field (Matt. 13:44), a merchant seeking beautiful pearls (Matt. 13:45-46), the foolish virgins who needed to buy oil for themselves (Matt. 25:1-13), and a man traveling into a far country who leaves his goods in the hands of his servants who are to do business on his behalf (Matt. 25:14-30). The lessons of forgiving others (Matt. 18:21-35) and the parable concerning the first and the last (Matt. 19:30-16) are illustrated by using monetary terms. Though other gospels do this to a lesser degree, these stories may suggest the personality of the author, giving weight to the traditional belief that Matthew is indeed the author of this gospel.

The Original Readers of Matthew's Gospel

One of the basic rules of good interpretation is to identify the intended readers for any given document. What is the message the author desires them to hear? Only when this is determined can the "Word of the Lord" be meaningful and applicable to any other generation or culture.

The first readers targeted by this gospel were obviously Jews. Matthew is replete with Jewish terms and titles. It is assumed that the readers are familiar with the Jewish ways and schools of thought. For example, Matthew does not need to explain the Jewish tradition of washing before eating:

> *"Then the scribes and Pharisees who were from Jerusalem came to Jesus, saying, 'Why do Your disciples transgress the tradition of the elders? For **they do not wash their hands when they eat bread.**' He answered and said to them, 'Why do you also transgress the commandments of God because of your tradition?'"* (Matt. 15:1-3)

The gospel of Mark records the same incident, but the author recognized the need to clarify the Jewish hand washing tradition for his Roman readers:

> *"Now when they saw some of His disciples eat bread with defiled, that is, with **unwashed hands**, they found fault. For the Pharisees and all the Jews do not eat unless they **wash their hands** in a special way, holding the tradition of the elders. When they come from the marketplace, **they do not eat unless they wash.** And there are many other things which they have received and hold, like the washing of cups, pitchers, copper vessels, and couches."* (Mark. 7:2-4)

11

(It is possible that since the author explains a few Jewish customs and words, such as releasing a prisoner at Passover (Matt. 27:15), that some of the readers are a fringe in Palestine rather than in Judea.)

To demonstrate that Jesus is indeed the fulfillment of all Jewish expectations, Matthew frequently quotes from the Old Testament scriptures. For example, consider the following:

> *"So all this was done that it might be fulfilled which was spoken by the Lord through the prophet, saying: **'Behold, the virgin shall be with child, and bear a Son, and they shall call His name Immanuel,'** which is translated, 'God with us.' "* (Matt. 1:22-23 – Isa. 7:14)

> *"Then was fulfilled what was spoken by Jeremiah the prophet, saying: **'A voice was heard in Ramah, Lamentation, weeping, and great mourning, Rachel weeping for her children,** Refusing to be comforted, Because they are no more.' "* (Matt. 2:17-18 – Jer. 31:15)

> *"And he came and dwelt in a city called Nazareth, that it might be fulfilled which was spoken by the prophets, **'He shall be called a Nazarene.'** "* (Matt. 2:23 – Isa. 11:1)

> *"And leaving Nazareth, He came and dwelt in Capernaum, which is by the sea, in the regions of Zebulun and Naphtali, that it might be fulfilled which was spoken by Isaiah the prophet, saying: **'The land of Zebulun and the land of Naphtali, By the way of the sea, beyond the Jordan, Galilee of the Gentiles: The people who sat in darkness have seen a great light, And upon those who sat in the region and shadow of death Light has dawned.'** "* (Matt. 4:13-16 – Isa. 9:1-2)

The life, ministry, death and resurrection of Christ are shown to be the fulfillment of all the prophetic hopes of the nation. The entire existence of Christ is demonstrated as agreeing with all of Israel's past. As one example, Matthew shows that just as the nation of Israel had been called out of Egypt many centuries earlier, so Christ is also out of Egypt (Matt. 2:15).

Matthew quotes one hundred and twenty-one prophecies, overwhelmingly proving that Jesus fulfilled the Old Testament expectations. By quoting these Old Testament scriptures, Matthew shows that Jesus is the long-expected and promised Messiah, the prophesied Servant of the Lord, the Savior, and the Son of David. The right of Jesus to this title is proven by His genealogy provided in Matt. 1:1-17. The circumstances concerning His birth are those of a king. By contrast, compare the genealogy of Christ written by Luke (Luke 3:23-38). There, the author's intent is to show that Jesus is identified with mankind in general, and thus his humanity is emphasized. While the birth of Jesus in Luke's gospel identifies Him with the poor, Matthew traces His ancestry through the royal lineage to show Jesus as king.

The miracles and teachings of Jesus fulfill all that the prophets foretold. He is proven to be the Son of Man, King, Christ, Servant, Chosen One, Elect, Righteous One, Son, and Bridegroom. All of these are well-known Jewish terms that express their hope in the coming Messiah. These prophecies are quoted according to the Jewish mind-set, often allegorizing in such a manner that it is difficult for other cultures to comprehend. Jesus is shown to have a mission to the lost sheep of the house of Israel (Matt. 10:6). Throughout the gospel, Matthew is responding to well-known Jewish misunderstandings regarding their Messiah.

Jesus' manner of teaching parallels the methods of the rabbinical schools. For instance, the rabbis often use a numerical arrangement of ideas, often triplets. The most common ones group together terms such as "ask, seek, and knock" (Matt. 7:7-8) and "almsgiving, prayer, and fasting" (Matt. 6:1-18). Twenty-four such triplets are found in Matthew.

There is no doubt that the author of this gospel is a Jew, and that he is writing to the Jews. However, this does not mean that he is pro-Jewish. He definitely wants to show the false position, beliefs and expectations of the nation of Israel.

The Brewing Conflict

It is impossible to pinpoint the exact date of the writing of this gospel. The evidence is not conclusive, but probably it was written prior to the destruction of the temple at Jerusalem in 70 A.D. Matthew does not speak of this horrible event as if it had happened already, but at the time of writing, he seems to anticipate it.

Tremendous insight into Matthew will be gained if the student of the gospel realizes that a clean break between Israel and the church was not yet complete. The first Christian church was considered a sect within Judaism, but it grew to be mostly a Gentile body outside of Judaism. Indeed, much of the conflict the early church encountered developed over the issue of how the Gentile converts were to relate to the Law of Moses and the political and religious economy of Israel in general.

Out of this conflict the Gentile church emerged, quite unrelated to the Law of Moses as the devout Jew understood it. To the Jew, this was a difficult, if not blasphemous, concept. At the start, Jewish believers in Christ remained in the highly Judaistic church and brought Jesus into their already established framework of thinking. A great conflict arose in their minds when they began to realize that this Christ that they had accepted was not in keeping with their traditional approach and interpretation of the Law of Moses. People in other generations and cultures cannot easily understand the great dilemma that the Jewish believer in Christ faced. This tension would be brought to its conclusion when the Roman army, under its commander Titus, totally destroyed the temple, as predicted by Jesus:

> *"Then Jesus went out and departed from the temple, and His disciples came up to show Him the buildings of the temple. And Jesus said to them, **'Do you not see all these things? Assuredly, I say to you, not one stone shall be left here upon another, that shall not be thrown down.'** "* (Matt. 24:1-2)

This great catastrophe was likely on Matthew's mind as he wrote to Jewish believers in Christ.

The Purpose of the Gospel

The break of the church from the trappings of Judaism is imminent. If the Jewish convert to Christ could not free his conscience from the faulty understanding of Israel's hopes, and if Christ is seen only as being incorporated into Judaism, then his entire scheme of faith in Christ would be overthrown at the temple's destruction. Matthew's task is not only to give evidence that Jesus is indeed the fulfillment of the Jewish hopes and expectations, but also to prove that the nation of Israel misunderstood the very nature of those very expectations. Their own view of the Law of Moses was faulty, and their ideas of the nature of the Messiah and the work He was to accomplish also needed adjustment. A terrible time of calamity is about to fall upon the nation of Israel. Matthew writes to prepare fellow believers in Christ for the prospect of a final and total break with the faith they had been taught since their childhood days. Matthew's aims are similar to those of the writer of the epistle to the Hebrews. The reader is left with the impression that the Jews are horrified at the thought of the destruction of Jerusalem and the sharp contention Jesus has with the scribes and Pharisees.

Matthew believes that there is yet time for the Jews to be won to Christ. There is a strong effort to convince his fellow Jews that Jesus is indeed the Messiah, and that their previous notions and concepts need to be changed.

Matthew has other concerns as he writes this gospel. The state of the church has deteriorated, and Matthew sounds many warnings. He warns the current generation by citing many examples of the failures of the previous generation that rejected Christ. He exposes the ignorance and blindness of the one in order to warn the next, so that they will not commit the same mistakes. The newer generation does not need to suffer rejection for its blindness and ignorance as well. Matthew draws together specific stories and sayings of Jesus to make that point. It should be noticed that Matthew does not present his material in strict chronological order. Instead he groups together stories and sayings that make the same theological point.

As an example of Matthew's arrangement of his material, follow the thoughts on God's relation to the house of Israel. In chapter 10, Christ is sent to the lost sheep of the house of Israel. Chapter 12 records two Sabbath controversies and a plot to kill Jesus. At this point, a total rejection of Jesus occurs in Matthew's arrangement, and Christ subsequently turns to the Gentiles. Chapter 13 records that after Jesus is rejected, He speaks in parables so that He cannot be understood. In chapter 21, He speaks of the kingdom of God being taken from them and given to another, and in chapter 23, He no longer refers to the temple as His Father's house but instead calls it "their" house. Obviously, because Matthew is unfolding a truth, he does not keep his material in strict chronological order. Rather he arranges it in doctrinal sequence.

Another concern fills Matthew's mind. Many of the Jewish believers in Christ have grown weary waiting for His return. Many of the parables told in this gospel deal with the return of Christ and emphasize a lengthy wait. This results in the cooling of their hearts and becoming alarmed at the state of the world.

Often a believer will exist on emotional ecstasy without giving proper attention to doctrinal foundations. When patience is subsequently required, the lack of foundation often reveals itself in evil behavior. The disappointment concerning the speedy return by Jesus easily led to the various evils that Matthew addresses. Matthew not only gives his prescription for the state of the heart but also many warnings to half-committed believers who claim a false assurance. Matthew believes that people can be self-deceived and have a presumptuous overconfidence. In Matthew's perception, the church has been adulterated and needs to be awakened out of its slumber. He speaks of wheat and tares, goats and sheep, bad and good fish, wise and unwise virgins, and those who know and do God's will and those who claim to do it.

In speaking of these concerns, Matthew gives tremendous insight into the very nature of the gospel and its effects upon the life of the believer. Some of the questions he answers are:

What is salvation? What part does repentance play?
What is the importance of living the Christian life?
Is righteous living to be evident as a result of believing in Christ?
What is grace?
What is the proper relationship of the believer to the Law of Moses?
How did Jesus interpret the Law?
How are believers to regard future judgment?
What is the church? (Only this gospel employs the term.)

What is conversion? What is discipleship?
What is the believer's proper attitude toward future hope?
What is the work of the church?
What is the necessity and nature of faith in the work of the Lord?
What is the kingdom of heaven?

Matthew brings all of these questions to bear upon the minds of his readers. He addresses these issues to a church that has hearts growing cool and is in danger of being completely shaken by the destruction of Jerusalem, the temple, and a final and total break with Judaism.

One more note concerning the arrangement of Matthew's material needs to be addressed. Outside of his narratives concerning the birth and death of Christ, all the material is arranged into five smaller books within the gospel. This is likely done to have the gospel written in the same style as the five books of Moses. Each book within the gospel contains a section of stories and a major discourse by Jesus. Some of the books also contain some shorter discourses of Jesus as well. Each book within the gospel ends with a statement such as the following: "Now it came to pass, when Jesus had finished these sayings." (Matt. 7:28; 11:1; 13:53; 19:1; 26:1).

Matthew has a great deal to say to the many succeeding generations since his first Jewish readers. A thorough study of Matthew will produce a foundation that will be unshakable in the worst of times, for that is its purpose to its original readers.

Thought Questions

1. Why was Matthew's inclusion among the twelve disciples likely to cause dissension?

2. Why do you think Jesus chose Matthew?

3. That Matthew wrote this gospel has never been disputed seriously. Does the content of this gospel suggest Matthew's authorship? Explain.

4. What makes you think that the Jews were the original readers of Matthew's gospel?

5. State a portion of Scripture that identifies Jesus as the fulfillment of all Jewish expectations.

6. Why does Matthew trace Jesus' ancestry through royal lineage?

7. What evidence do we have that Matthew wrote this gospel prior to 70 A.D.?

8. What was Matthew's primary purpose in writing his gospel?

The Times and World of Matthew

Chapter Two

Judah ceased to be an independent nation six hundred years prior to the birth of Christ and had been subjected to the Babylonians, Persians, Greeks, and finally the Romans. How could Israel, continuously dominated by heathen and godless empires, keep its distinctive nature as an independent nation founded upon the laws of God as revealed through Moses?

Interpreters of the Law

Like the writers of the other gospels, Matthew records the denial of Christ by the leaders of Israel and, consequently, the rejection of Israel by Christ. The Pharisees especially, along with the Sadducees, scribes, chief priests and elders, are shown to be in bitter opposition to Jesus, and Jesus denounces them in no uncertain terms:

> *"For I say to you, that unless your righteousness exceeds the righteousness of the scribes and Pharisees, **you will by no means enter the kingdom of heaven.**"* (Matt. 5:20)

> *"Hypocrites! Well did Isaiah prophesy about you, saying: '**These people draw near to Me with their mouth, And honor Me with their lips, But their heart is far from Me,** And in vain they worship Me, Teaching as doctrines the commandments of men.'"* (Matt. 15:7-9)
> Read: Matt. 16:6; 23:13-39

These religious leaders were directly responsible for the death of Christ, as indicated below:

*"Then the Pharisees went out and **plotted against Him, how they might destroy Him.**"* (Matt. 12:14)

*"From that time Jesus began to show to His disciples that He must go to Jerusalem, and **suffer many things from the elders and chief priests and scribes, and be killed,** and be raised the third day."* (Matt. 16:21)

*"Behold, we are going up to Jerusalem, and the Son of Man will be betrayed to the chief priests and to the scribes; and **they will condemn Him to death, and deliver Him to the Gentiles to mock and to scourge and to crucify.** And the third day He will rise again."* (Matt. 20:18-19) Read: Matt. 26:3-5; 27:1-2; 28:11-15.

On several occasions, they attempted to entangle Jesus in His own talk in order to lay a charge against Him. However, their efforts were always unsuccessful:

*"Then the Pharisees went and plotted how they might entangle Him in His talk. And they sent to Him their disciples with the Herodians, saying, 'Teacher, we know that You are true, and teach the way of God in truth; nor do You care about anyone, for You do not regard the person of men. Tell us, therefore, what do you think? **Is it lawful to pay taxes to Caesar, or not?'** But Jesus perceived their wickedness, and said, 'Why do you test Me, you hypocrites? Show Me the tax money.' So they brought Him a denarius. And He said to them, 'Whose image and inscription is this?' They said to Him, 'Caesar's.' And He said to them, '**Render therefore to Caesar the things that are Caesar's, and to God the things***

that are God's. *' When they had heard these words, they marveled, and left Him and went their way.''* (Matt. 22:15-22) Read. Matt. 12:38; 16:1; 19:3; 22:23.

At other times the religious leaders used outright sarcasm. Examples of this are found in Matt. 9:32-34; 12:24; 21:23. They had accused Jesus of casting out demons by the power of Beelzebub. This kind of treatment by the Pharisees and Sadducees demonstrated the justice of the scorching remarks of John the Baptist when he called them a brood of vipers (Matt. 3:7).

Why did these various groups oppose Jesus so vehemently? Why did they not recognize the promised Messiah when He finally arrived? How could they so completely misunderstand His mission and not only reject Him, but also crucify Him?

For four hundred years prior to His incarnation, a period between the Old and New Testaments known as the silent years, there was no prophetic voice of the Lord, and the hearts of His people were slipping away from Him. Judah ceased to be an independent nation six hundred years prior to the birth of Christ and had been subjected to the Babylonians, Persians, Greeks, and finally the Romans. How could Israel, continuously dominated by heathen and godless empires, keep its distinctive nature as an independent nation founded upon the laws of God as revealed through Moses? Many different ways were sought to preserve the Jewish heritage, resulting in various schools of thought.

During the two centuries before Christ was born, several very different sects developed within Judaism. What were the characteristics of each? A brief discussion of each of the sects follows.

The **Pharisees**, founded as a protest movement against the increasingly strong Hellenistic (Greek) influence, was the sect most openly hostile to Jesus. They felt that the Israelites were becoming more like their heathen conquerors and protested loudly against the deterioration of their own laws. Therefore, they insisted upon even minute observance of every jot and tittle of the law as they understood it. More will be said about their interpretation of the law.

The **Sadducees**, by contrast, made peace with their political conquerors and leaders. As a result, they were rewarded with positions of wealth and influence. They were 'appointed' by the political rulers to the positions of high priest and temple administration. Since the Romans recognized them as both political and religious leaders, they became wealthy aristocrats, keeping themselves aloof from and unpopular with the masses. They recognized only the five books of Moses (Genesis through Deuteronomy) as inspired and rejected the writings of the prophets. Their faith was largely a series of negations:

> *"Then some Sadducees, **who say there is no resurrection,** came to Him; and they asked Him, saying:"* (Mark 12:18)

> *"For the Sadducees say that there is no resurrection – **and no angel or spirit;** but the Pharisees confess both."* (Acts. 23:8)

The **Herodians** were Jews of influence, being supporters of Herod who granted them many concessions in order to win their favor. The greatest gift he gave the Jews was the massive temple. Since the Herodians backed the ruling family of Herod, they indirectly supported the Romans who gave Herod his authority.

The **Zealots** were extreme patriots who were determined to resist Rome at any cost. Their fanaticism brought the Roman army under General Titus to Jerusalem in 70 A.D. There, he leveled

Jerusalem and destroyed its beloved temple. By this act, Israel ceased to be a nation.

The **Essenes**, not directly mentioned in the gospels, had an even stronger reaction than the Pharisees did to the disrespect for the Jewish laws: they withdrew from society to form their own "monasteries." Though they had extremely high morals, they were very legalistic and ascetic. Some of their "order" did not permit marriage or even the touching of a woman. They performed manual labor, and adhered to strict discipline and rigid laws. Some have thought that John the Baptist may have belonged to this sect, but there is no convincing evidence that John was an Essene.

The Pharisees became the formalists of their day, the Sadducees the free thinkers, and the Essenes the puritans. Though they each developed a different view of their problem, they did have some common ground. They looked for a national restoration of Israel and for the exaltation of their nation over the entire world. Their view was purely political and external. There was absolutely no concept of the Messiah dying to atone for sin, and they were not interested in a "spiritual" kingdom as Jesus preached. Even the disciples of Jesus showed bewilderment at some of His sayings.

These groups clashed with Jesus over almost every matter regarding the Law's interpretation. They viewed its purpose differently; consequently, they argued about its proper application. In showing Jesus' response to their accusations, Matthew was instructing his readers in the proper interpretation of the Law. He knew the heart condition of his original readers and understood their need of correction. Matthew revealed the proper role of the Law in the economy of God and the believer's relationship to it. He described the character of the Christian life and the manner in which one enters into it.

It is difficult for others to grasp the importance of the Law of Moses to the nation of Israel. The entire nation was founded upon the Law; therefore, the interpretation of the Law influenced the whole structure of the nation and life as the Jews knew it. The implementation of Jesus' interpretation of the Law would bring drastic changes to the Jewish society. This was no small matter.

Thought Questions

1. Why was the Law so important to the Jewish people?

2. Why did these various groups oppose Jesus so vehemently?

3. Contrast the viewpoints of the Pharisees and the Sadducees.

4. Concerning their expectations of the Messiah, what common ground was there among the Pharisees, Sadducees and Essenes?

5. Why did the leaders of Israel not recognize the promised Messiah when He finally arrived?

6. How could the leaders so completely misunderstand His mission and not only reject Him, but also crucify Him?

Interpreters of the Law

Chapter Three

Through a changed heart and the Law written by the Holy Spirit as a life-principle on its tables, the believer is assured that he "shall not covet." These words are translated from a command into a promise.

Clashing with the Pharisees

More than any other gospel writer, Matthew recorded the debates Jesus had with the Pharisees. Jesus condemned their viewpoint concerning the Law and certainly did not encourage them to greater sincerity. However, He urged them to strive toward a true insight into its intent. Nicodemus was sincere, but wrong (John 3); likewise, Joseph of Arimathaea and Saul of Tarsus had misinterpreted the Law. Jesus challenged their official rulings (Matt. 15:1-9). Many drew Him into discussions on debatable points (Matt. 19:3-9), but He repeatedly warned against their teaching (Matt. 16:1-12) and set His interpretation against their prevailing views (Matt. 5:21-48).

In order to maintain their distinction as a nation founded and set apart by God at Mt. Sinai with the giving of the Ten Commandments (Ex. 19-20), the Pharisees sought to explain the Law in light of their present situation. Being a conquered people, they experienced new circumstances and different influences. In the face of these new surroundings, they queried how the Law of

Moses applied to their nation. How could the Sabbath day be observed and kept holy? What is holiness? The Pharisees attempted to make the Law applicable to everyday life, a noble effort in itself, yet dangerous if the interpretation and application is incorrect! This danger is not something unique to the Pharisees only; it has often been repeated by many generations since.

With the "sincere" desire to make the Law workable in the changing culture of the Greek-Roman world, the Pharisees developed systems of tradition that sought to make the Law workable in a variety of circumstances. Tradition began as a commentary on the Law, but ultimately it was raised to the level of the Law itself. Tradition, otherwise known as the oral law, became known as the "Mishna," while the written Law was called the "Torah." In time, tradition became more important than the original Law of Moses, because the Pharisees argued that it affected the life of the ordinary man more intimately than the remote written Law of Moses.

Unfortunately, the Pharisees missed the whole nature and purpose of the Law. While Jesus summed up the whole Law as love (Matt. 22:37-40; 12:7; 9:13), the spiritual meaning was lost to these erring interpreters. However, within the Pharisaic interpretation of the Law there existed different schools of thought, such as the opposing schools of Hillel and Shammai. These two schools of thought differed, for instance, on the subject of divorce. Sometimes, one school of thought was closer to the truth than the other.

> *"Then one of the scribes came, and having heard them reasoning together, perceiving that He had answered them well, asked Him, 'Which is the first commandment of all?' Jesus answered him, 'The first of all the commandments is: Hear, O Israel, the Lord our God, the Lord is one. And you shall love the Lord your God with*

all your heart, with all your soul, with all your mind, and with all your strength. This is the first commandment. And the second, like it, is this: 'You shall love your neighbor as yourself.' There is no other commandment greater than these.' So the scribe said to Him, 'Well said, Teacher. **You have spoken the truth, for there is one God, and there is no other but He. And to love Him with all the heart, with all the understanding, with all the soul, and with all the strength, and to love one's neighbor as oneself, is more than all the whole burnt offerings and sacrifices.' Now when Jesus saw that he answered wisely, He said to him, 'You are not far from the kingdom of God.'** *But after that no one dared question Him.*" (Mark 12:28-34)

The oral law of the Pharisees became more complicated and full of minute observances, which, according to Jesus, worked against the whole intent and purpose of the Law. A prime example is the clash Jesus had with them over the washing of their hands (Matt. 15:1-20). Jesus was not afraid to publicly call them hypocrites, nothing but stage actors who were playing a part, pretending to be something they really weren't. They, according to Jesus, were blind fools (Matt. 15:7,14; 23:13-33). Some quick observances of the extremes to which they took their application will demonstrate the foolishness of their position. They majored on the legislation of externals. Many of their traditions, for instance, dealt with the observance of the Sabbath: the definitions of holiness and work; the type of work one could do on the Sabbath without desecrating it.

The Mishna (tradition or oral law, the commentary of the written Law to supposedly make it applicable to everyday life) was divided into six sections. The second section is divided further into twelve divisions, and all twelve of them are devoted to rules regarding the Sabbath.

31

The first rule concerns the definition of labor. After all, had not Jeremiah said that work on the Sabbath was not to be done?

> *"Thus says the Lord: 'Take heed to yourselves, and bear no burden on the Sabbath day, nor bring it in by the gates of Jerusalem; nor carry a burden out of your houses on the Sabbath day, **nor do any work**, but hallow the Sabbath day, as I commanded your fathers."* (Jer. 17:21,22)

The most common kind of labor was to carry something. The definition of carrying was then divided into eight ordinances. The bearing of a burden was divided into two separate acts: lifting up and then putting down. If an object were lifted up, answers to the following questions had to be determined: Was it lifted from a private place or a public place? Was it to be put down in the same place or a different place? Was that place private or public? What, indeed, was the definition of private and public? The reasoning went on and on.

No wonder Jesus looked at the multitudes and saw them weary and heavy-laden, needing rest for their souls (Matt. 11:28-30). The people of God did not exhibit joy; the lives of the Israelites were burdened with ceaseless, minute, external observances that only served to wear out the nation.

Instead of leading to spirituality, legalism led to arrogance, pride, and haughtiness on the part of the Pharisees. Without any regard for the inner meaning or intent of the Law, the letter of the Law produced a system of works that touched the external things only and demanded unyielding submission from the people's self-efforts. Righteousness was understood in terms of externals, and a proud Pharisee could "display" his false religious righteousness before an unsuspecting world of observers (Matt. 6:1-18).

All through the gospel of Matthew, Jesus taught that holiness and righteousness could not be attained simply by legislation of outward things only. He continually emphasized that a radical change of heart was needed. Jesus did not discard the external Law but rather fulfilled and established its true nature. Its purpose was to reveal sin and to expose the hardness of man's heart. Only through a change in the inner nature of man, by receiving a new heart, could the righteousness that the Law required be fulfilled. While the Pharisees only applied the Law as a system of externals, Jesus saw it as something to be revealed upon the tables of a man's heart.

According to Jesus, the Law was given to teach love for God and neighbor:

> *"Jesus said to him, '***You shall love the Lord your God with all your heart, with all your soul, and with all your mind. This is the first and great commandment. And the second is like it: You shall love your neighbor as yourself.*** On these two commandments hang all the Law and the Prophets.' "* (Matt. 22:37-40)

The method of interpretation by both the Pharisees and the Sadducees was a leaven that was to be avoided (Matt. 16:1-12). It is too easy to reduce spirituality to an external code of behavior by which some are condemned and others become haughty. All too often that code of ethics is not consistent with the nature of God and is divorced from His heart and purposes. To be spiritual, one must know God in a personal relationship.

Jesus and the Intent of the Law

On many occasions, the Pharisees sought to prove that Jesus was a sinner by demonstrating that He and His disciples broke the Law. However, this worked against them as Jesus maintained that though He violated their interpretation of the Law, known as the Mishna, He was still true to the Law of Moses. Jesus merely broke their erroneous interpretation of the Law. Throughout his gospel, Matthew revealed Jesus as completely righteous in the correct light of the Law, while exposing the faulty Pharisees' approach. This was one of Matthew's aims in writing his gospel, and it was very important that his intended readers understand this point. The school of interpretation invented by the Pharisees would be abolished in 70 A.D. when the Romans destroyed the city of Jerusalem and, along with it, their beloved temple.

Jesus' teaching was so different from the prevailing view of the day, so vastly dissimilar to that of the scribes and Pharisees, that it led people to inquire about the position Jesus took concerning the Law of Moses. Obviously, they understood that Jesus was opposed to their tradition, the Pharisees' interpretation of the Law. According to the Jewish framework of thinking, the multitudes wondered whether Jesus intended to overthrow piety and holiness, and, by putting morality ahead of the ceremonial, to repudiate the Levitical system. Since He was a friend of sinners, was He opposed to the Law? Was he a heretic? As stated in Matthew 7:28-29, He did not teach as the scribes:

> *"And so it was, when Jesus had ended these sayings, that the people were astonished at His teaching, **for He taught them as one having authority, and not as the scribes.**"*

Jesus' answer strongly stated His position regarding the Law. He came to fulfill it, not by supplementation, but by meeting its demands, by offering to God what it requires, and by magnifying it:

> *"Do not think that I came to destroy the Law or the Prophets. I did not come to destroy but to fulfill. For assuredly, I say to you, till heaven and earth pass away,* **one jot or one tittle will by no means pass from the law till all is fulfilled.** *Whoever therefore breaks one of the least of these commandments, and teaches men so, shall be called least in the kingdom of heaven; but whoever does and teaches them, he shall be called great in the kingdom of heaven. For I say to you, that unless your righteousness exceeds the righteousness of the scribes and Pharisees, you will by no means enter the kingdom of heaven."* (Matt. 5:17-20)

The gospel is not an abrogation of the Law. None of its righteous demands are rescinded. Rather, the gospel and the Law agree. Grace establishes the moral righteousness of the Law:

> *"Do we then make void the law through faith? Certainly not! On the contrary,* **we establish the law.***"* (Rom. 3:31)

The gospel is the Law 'Written on the Heart':

> *"For this is the covenant that I will make with the house of Israel after those days, says the Lord: I will put My laws in their mind and* **write them on their hearts***; and I will be their God, and they shall be My People."* (Heb. 8:10)

Rather than being abandoned, the Law becomes a life-principle operating in a new heart. Note the phrase "cause you" in Ezekiel's prophecy:

> *"I will give you a new heart and put a new spirit within you; I will take the heart of stone out of your flesh and give you a heart of flesh. I will put My Spirit within you and **cause you** to walk in My statutes, and you will keep My judgments and do them."* (Ezek. 36:26-27)

The keeping and doing of God's judgments is due to the Spirit put within the believer. When viewed properly, the inner man delights in the Law of God. The Pharisees had no true comprehension of the nature of God. They did not appreciate the morality of the Law; thus, they saw only the letter of the Law and produced a system of interpretation that was mainly a series of negations.

By observing Jesus' denouncements of the Pharisaic view of the Law, we can discern that their concept of righteousness widely missed the mark. Matthew 23 offers many comments on this.

Firstly, their righteousness was external and had nothing whatever to do with the heart (c.f. Matt. 23:25-28):

> *"Woe to you, scribes and Pharisees, hypocrites! For you cleanse the outside of the cup and the dish, but inside they are full of extortion and self-indulgence. Blind Pharisee, first cleanse the inside of the cup and dish, that the outside of them may be clean also. Woe to you, scribes and Pharisees, hypocrites! **For you are like whitewashed tombs which indeed appear beautiful outwardly, but inside are full of dead men's bones and all uncleanness. Even so you also outwardly appear***

righteous to men, but inside you are full of hypocrisy and lawlessness."

This contrast between Jesus' and the religious leaders' viewpoints is also strikingly brought out in Matthew 5:17-48 and 15:1-20.

Secondly, their righteousness was only partial, observing the ceremonial with no regard for the moral aspects of the Law. Matthew 23:23 makes this plain:

"Woe to you, scribes and Pharisees, hypocrites! **For you pay tithe of mint and anise and cummin, and have neglected the weightier matters of the law: justice and mercy and faith.** *These you ought to have done, without leaving the others undone."*

Thirdly, because everything was outward, the Pharisees became proud, with their motivation becoming that of self-interest. Matt. 6:1-18 and the following scripture make this clear:

*"**But all their works they do to be seen by men.** They make their phylacteries broad and enlarge the borders of their garments. They love the best places at feasts, the best seats in the synagogues, greetings in the marketplaces, and to be called by men, 'Rabbi, Rabbi.' "* (Matt. 23:5-7)

This contrast concerning the definition of righteousness is powerfully brought forth to the reader in Matt. 5:21-48. When using the recurring statement "You have heard that it was said of those of old.... But I say to you," Jesus is not contrasting Himself with Moses. "Those of old" refers to the ancients, meaning the scribes and the Pharisees from previous generations. Jesus does not denounce the Law of Moses; here, He rescues it from the perversion of the blind leaders of Israel. In these verses, the corrupt interpretations of the commands of Moses are put forth, and then Jesus gives the true understanding as revealed in the nature of God. When He is accused of breaking the Law, Jesus demonstrates His innocence by revealing the faulty handling of the Law by the scribes and Pharisees. In so answering, He expounds the proper light in which to view the Law.

Three principles may be found in Matthew's gospel.

Firstly, righteousness is never achieved by outward legislation. Righteousness is an internal matter; it is a matter of the heart. This was made plain in Matt. 15:1-20. Moses and the prophets said this, but somehow the religious leaders missed the point. Read Deut. 5:29; 30:6; Jer. 17:9-10; Ps. 40:6-8, where it is stated that the law was to be imposed on the heart of man. This does not imply that outward behavior and ethics are unimportant; but as Matt. 23:26 demonstrates, the gospel gives a new heart which then leads to a new character lived outwardly. This is a working out of the truth of Prov. 4:23: the issues of life proceed from the heart, a statement that Matt. 12:34-35 echoes:

> *"Brood of vipers! How can you, being evil, speak good things? For out of the abundance of the heart the mouth speaks. **A good man out of the good treasure of his heart brings forth good things,** and an evil man out of the evil treasure brings forth evil things."*

Secondly, to interpret the Law, the intent of the Law must be recognized. Regarding Moses' allowing a divorce decree, Jesus takes His inquirers back to God's original purpose (Matt. 19: 1-12). What has been the desire of God from the beginning? In this case, the Pharisees wrongly stated that Moses gave a "command" for divorce. Jesus corrects that attitude by discussing the motive and intent of God, and then in light of that intent, because of the hardness of men's hearts, He declares that Moses "permitted" divorce. A woman may suffer abuse and have her life threatened if the husband has no intention, due to the hardness of his own heart, to correct his life. For this reason, Moses allowed divorce.

Thirdly, God gave the Law to express His love and to show how love will be lived out in a sinful world. This is the express teaching of Matt. 22:36-40 and the following scripture:

> "*Therefore,* **whatever you want men to do to you, do also to them,** *for this is the Law and the Prophets.*" (Matt. 7:12)

In the first four of the Ten Commandments, the believer is taught how honor and love for God is expressed. The remaining six commandments demonstrate how love for the neighbor and fellow man is recognized in a sinful society. What was a command in the Old Covenant, by the presence and agency of the Holy Spirit, now becomes a promise. For instance, the Old Covenant demanded outwardly of the believer not to covet. Now, through a changed heart and the Law written by the Spirit as a life-principle on its tables, the believer is assured that he "shall not covet." The very same words are translated from a command into a promise!

More needs to be said about knowing the intent of the Law. Even in modern courts, it is all too common to interpret the letter of a law apart from its intent. By doing this, as was the case of the scribes and Pharisees, the interpretation of the Law may betray its original meaning. The Pharisees failed in not having an accurate knowledge of the character of God. To them, the Law itself was the highest revelation that man could experience. It was the ultimate revelation for all time. Unfortunately, that whole premise was wrong and produced an erroneous basis upon which to build. Consequently, they created a method of understanding that did not begin with the nature of God Himself. Without this knowledge, they had no foundation upon which to properly assess or apply the Law. In so doing, they actually twisted the sense of the Law and worked against its true meaning. By this, they actually shut up the kingdom of heaven against men as stated in Matt. 23:13:

> *"But woe to you, scribes and Pharisees, hypocrites!* ***For you shut up the kingdom of heaven against men; for you neither go in yourselves, nor do you allow those who are entering to go in.****"*

In the words of Luke, they took away the key of knowledge, not entering the kingdom of heaven themselves, or allowing others to enter in (Luke 11:52). They became blind leaders of the blind (Matt. 15:14; 23:16). They interpreted the letter of the Law as paramount without any regard for its intent as revealed in the character of God Himself.

Without righteousness as revealed by the Law, liberty would quickly degenerate into license and turn to chaos. Millions of people in the modern era enjoy the privilege of driving a car, but without traffic laws, such a privilege could not be possible. Utter destruction would reign if the flow of traffic were not regulated. Likewise, liberty in Christ would end in many heresies and harmful practices if the righteousness of the Law were not produced as a life-principle upon the tables of a regenerated heart! Freedom from the outward Law is only possible because the Law is revealed inwardly as righteousness.

The purpose of the Law is to save life in a sinful world. Suppose someone has a serious accident and needs medical attention immediately. Life is hanging in the balance. Under such conditions, the letter of the law gives way to the intent of the law, allowing the ambulance operator to drive in excess of the speed limit, sometimes with a police escort. In such a case, the emergency driver is guiltless, for he is governed by the intent of the law, which is to preserve life. Since the law must be interpreted in light of its intent and purpose, in the case being considered, the emergency driver has to follow the intent of the law in order not to defeat its purpose.

Unless the believer starts with knowledge of God - His nature and love - the righteousness of the Law will be mishandled, creating a system of interpretation and application that misses the whole point, actually working against righteousness. This is very easily done. The Law of God, as expressed in the Ten Commandments and its various applications throughout the Law of Moses, needs to be seen in light of the character of God and not to be viewed as an end in itself.

Thought Questions

1. Consider the Apostle Paul's pharisaic religious heritage (Phil. 3:4-7). It is stated that.... *"As for Saul, he made havoc of the church, entering every house, and dragging off men and women, committing them to prison." (Acts 8:3).* How could the great Apostle Paul have committed these horrendous deeds?

2. Discuss the difference between the "Mishna" and the "Torah."

3. "Without any regard for the inner meaning or intent of the Law, the letter of the law (Pharisaic interpretation) produced a system of works that touched external things only." Explain.

4. Discuss Matthew's three major criticisms of the Pharisaic view of righteousness.

5. "Liberty in Christ would end in many heresies and harmful practices if the righteousness of the Law were not produced as a life-principle upon the tables of the heart." Discuss.

Section II.

The Gospel from Matthew's Perspective

Section II

Chapter Four

> *God's promise in the New Covenant is to write His laws, not on tables of stone, but on the tables of a new heart which He would give man. The New Covenant does not do away with righteousness, but it empowers man by giving him a new heart, causing God's laws to be internalized within man.*

The Gospel

Matthew's understanding of the gospel was the same as that preached by the prophets of old. Indeed, it was identical to the message of Jeremiah and Ezekiel. For instance, Jeremiah prophesied:

> *"Behold, the days are coming, says the Lord, when I will make a new covenant with the house of Israel and with the house of Judah – not according to the covenant I made with their fathers in the day that I took them by the hand to lead them out of the land of Egypt, My covenant which they broke, though I was husband to them, says the Lord. But this is the covenant that I will make with the house of Israel after those days, says the Lord: **I will put My law in their minds, and write it on their hearts; and I will be their God, and they shall be My people.** No more shall every man teach his neighbor, and every man his brother, saying, 'Know the Lord,' for they shall know Me, from the least of them to the greatest of them, says the Lord. **For I will forgive their iniquity, and their sin I will remember no more.**"* (Jer. 31:31-34)

Ezekiel fully concurs. In one of many prophetic utterances, he states:

> *"I will give you a new heart and put a new spirit within you; I will take the heart of stone out of your flesh and give you a heart of flesh.* **I will put My Spirit within you and cause you to walk in My statutes, and you will keep My judgments and do them.***"* (Ezek. 36:26-27)

According to the prophets, man's problem is his heart. He sins because of a deficient heart. The outflow from a man's heart exhibits how he thinks, speaks and acts. If the heart is wrong, the man is wrong. There are numerous scriptures scattered throughout the Old Testament that teach this same principle. A few examples are Jer. 17:1,9-10; Prov. 4:23; 23:7; Is. 29:13. In regeneration, the aim of the gospel is to effect a change in the heart of man. Only when that occurs can a righteousness that honors God be embraced and lived out.

The reason the Old Covenant, given through Moses, ended in dismal failure is that the heart of man could not render the obedience God required. Man, with sin engraved on the tables of his heart, simply cannot be pleasing to God. The heart is not inclined that way. Even though a man may wish to please God, he does not have the power to execute that desire. The gospel must radically change the nature of a man's heart.

During the time of the Old Covenant, the Law was written on tables of stone, totally external to the nature of man. God's promise in the New Covenant is to write His Laws, not on tables of stone, but on the tables of a new heart which He would give man. The New Covenant does not do away with righteousness, but it empowers man by giving him a new heart, causing God's laws to be internalized within him.

The Laws written on the tables of the heart do not refer to ceremonial rites that were typical of the tabernacle and its services. These offerings and sacrifices were a temporal necessity to "cover" man's sin until the promised Redeemer could actually remove it by the shedding of His blood. After Christ appeared, there was no need for the shadow any longer. The Pharisees, along with the other sects within Judaism, erred in their comprehension of the temporal nature of the tabernacle and its services. Their concept of the Law, except for a devout few such as Nicodemus and Joseph of Arimathaea, was almost exclusively external in outlook. They were not interested in the nature of man's heart and put their trust entirely in externals.

The Law to which the prophets such as Jeremiah and Ezekiel referred was not ceremonial rites; it was the truth that reflects the nature and mind of God. The Law is the righteousness for which the Ten Commandments stand; it is morality that is consistent with God Himself, and proceeds from Him. This is the Law that, as a result of coming under the sound of the gospel, is written on the tables of a man's heart.

This understanding of the Law caused the many clashes between Jesus and the Pharisees. Over and over again, Matthew, in the same vein as the prophets of old, declares that the heart of man is the problem, and that Christ came to radically change man right at that point. It is the pure in heart that will see God (Matt. 5:8). Adultery proceeds from the heart (Matt. 5:28). Evil communication proceeds from an evil heart (Matt. 5:37). A man speaks out of the abundance of his heart, and that which is in his heart will be drawn out of it (Matt. 12:34-35). The heart has grown dull (Matt. 13:15). Though a man may appear to approach God with externals, inwardly the heart may be far from Him (Matt. 15:8). It is not externals that defile a man, but the evil things that proceed from his heart (Matt. 15:18-20).

Matthew's preaching is the same as Jeremiah's: sin is engraved on the heart, and the gospel must effect a change there.

The gospel does not do away with the righteousness of the Law. When the Law is applied to the sinful heart of man, he is convicted inwardly of his condition before a holy God. This brings forth the fruit of repentance, which is contrition wrought within the heart. Repentance is taught strongly throughout Matthew's gospel and is shown to be the first step of man's deliverance from his stony heart in order to receive the pliable heart of flesh Ezekiel prophesied. The Beatitudes (Matt. 5:3-12) are simply the changes that take place in the heart as the Law is being written on it. The Beatitudes demonstrate the fruit of the repentance that yields the righteousness, proceeding from the heart, which is pleasing to God.

In this manner, the teaching of Jesus contrasted sharply with the interpretation of the scribes and Pharisees. According to Jesus, the Law is to teach the nature of God, and as a consequence, it must endure forever. It will never pass away (Matt. 5:17-19). The Law 'Written on the Heart' will teach a man to love God and his neighbor (Matt. 22:37-40). Love is seen as the fulfilling of the Law and as the nature of God Himself. Jesus demonstrates that the love of God was the motivation for the giving of His Laws, and the Laws of God are expressions of His love in a sinful world. Thus the gospel actually produces a change in man, as his heart is changed from stone to flesh, affecting a difference in behavior, speech and action. The love of God is reproduced in a new heart. All of this is brought about by faith in Christ Jesus, who by His Spirit works these changes in all who call on the name of the Lord.

In presenting the gospel in this manner, Matthew gives the true nature and value of the Law and shows how faith in Christ establishes righteousness in the life of the believer in Christ as testified by the prophets of old.

The Attack on Jesus

Jesus often violated the Pharisees' interpretation of the Law. His behavior did not conform to the Mishna, their interpretation of the written Law. The "tradition of the elders" had accumulated over the years as their commentary on Moses. Its purposes were to interpret the "obscure" written Law for everyday life and to preserve the nation of Israel as distinct from the rest of the world.

When Jesus was accused of breaking the Law, Matthew demonstrated that He was not guilty of violating the commands of God. In the many stories that Matthew recorded, Jesus showed that the Pharisaic interpretation missed the point. Though Jesus did not follow their interpretation and transgressed their traditions, He was not guilty of breaking the Law of God. When confrontations occurred, Jesus did not hesitate to point out how hypocritical and self-serving their interpretations are! He also showed that their interpretations contradicted and transgressed Moses!

The enemies of Christ attacked Jesus on four different fronts.

First, they had to account for His ability to perform the miraculous. This in itself drew many large crowds and gave Jesus an audience. The Pharisees attributed the miraculous to Satan and declared Jesus to be one of his representatives.

"As they went out, behold, they brought Him a man, mute and demon-possessed. And when the demon was cast out, the mute spoke. And the multitudes marveled, saying, 'It was never seen like this in Israel!' But the

Pharisees said, 'He casts out demons by the ruler of the demons.' " (Matt. 9:32-34. See also12:22-24.)

The Pharisees hoped their statement would turn His signs into an argument against Him and also would justify their resistance to Him. Formerly, this argument had a measure of success in causing some of the masses to turn from John the Baptist (Matt. 11:16-18).

Secondly, through answers He would give to cleverly planned questions, they tried to force Jesus into a compromising position. A prime example occurred when they asked Jesus whether or not taxes should be paid to Caesar (Matt. 22:15-22). A "yes" answer would alienate Him from the masses that despised paying Roman taxes, and a "no" reply would permit them to report Him to the Romans for trial. Jesus answered them:

*"Tell us, therefore, what do You think? **Is it lawful to pay taxes to Caesar, or not?** But Jesus perceived their wickedness, and said, 'Why do you test Me, you hypocrites? Show Me the tax money.' So they brought Him a denarius. And He said to them, 'Whose image and inscription is this?' They said to Him, 'Caesar's.' And He said to them, '**Render therefore to Caesar the things that are Caesar's, and to God the things that are God's.**' When they heard these words, they marveled, and left Him and went their way."* (Matt. 22:17-22)

Thirdly, Jesus was constantly accused of being a sinner. If this could be established, then obviously Jesus was not the Messiah; rather, He was a deceiver who misled the people. Then it would be the duty of the religious sects within Judaism to expose and arrest Him. Being persuaded that Jesus was a sinner, the Pharisees attempted on numerous occasions to establish this fact. Often, in the context of this third method of attack on Jesus, the discussion of the true nature of the Law is found. Jesus consistently rejected their interpretation of the Law, and as the stories were told, it became apparent that the entire scheme of interpretation of the Pharisees and other religious groups was faulty. Two Sabbath stories are good examples of this (Matt. 12:1-14):

> *"At that time Jesus went through the grainfields on the Sabbath. And His disciples were hungry, and began to pluck heads of grain and to eat. And when the Pharisees saw it, they said to Him,* **'Look, Your disciples are doing what is not lawful to do on the Sabbath!'** *But He said to them, 'Have you not read what David did when he was hungry, he and those who were with him: how he entered the house of God and ate the showbread which was not lawful for him to eat, nor for those who were with him, but only for the priests?* **Or have you not read in the law that on the Sabbath the priests in the temple profane the Sabbath, and are blameless?** *Yet I say to you that in this place there is One greater than the temple. But if you had known what this means, I desire mercy and not sacrifice, you would not have condemned the guiltless. For the Son of Man is Lord even of the Sabbath.' "* (Matt. 12:1-8)

Fourthly, in a rare move that brought Pharisees and Sadducees together, Jesus was charged with claiming equality with God. To this the Pharisees cried out, "Blasphemy!" and the Sadducees saw a movement where excitable, superstitious, and ignorant people would be led away. If unchecked, this would eventually bring Roman persecution and result in the loss of any remaining sense of national independence. This, indeed, became the very charge for which Jesus was crucified.

Though the third charge against Jesus is the one that dealt directly with the proper interpretation of the Law, Matthew gives only one answer that will satisfy all who would doubt the claims of Jesus. Matthew constantly points to faith in the person of Christ (Matt. 16:13-20):

*"When Jesus came into the region of Caesarea Philippi, He asked His disciples, saying, 'Who do men say that I, the Son of Man, am?' So they said, 'Some say John the Baptist, some Elijah, and others Jeremiah or one of the prophets.' He said to them, 'But who do you say that I am?' Simon Peter answered and said, **'You are the Christ, the Son of the living God.'** Jesus answered and said to him, **'Blessed are you, Simon Bar-Jonah, for flesh and blood has not revealed this to you, but My Father who is in heaven. And I also say to you that you are Peter, and on this rock I will build My church, and the gates of Hades shall not prevail against it.** And I will give you the keys of the kingdom of heaven, and whatever you bind on earth will be bound in heaven, and whatever you loose on earth will be loosed in heaven.' Then He commanded His disciples that they should tell no one that **He was Jesus the Christ.**"*

Jesus is the Christ, the Son of the living God. To have this revealed by the living God is to dispel all fears and doubts.

Thought Questions

1. Interpret Jeremiah's statement in Jeremiah 17:9-10:

    "The heart is deceitful above all things, And desperately wicked; Who can know it? I, the Lord, search the heart, I test the mind, Even to give every man according to his ways, According to the fruit of his doings."

2. During the Old Covenant, where was the Law written?

3. What is considered to be the first step of man's deliverance from his stony heart?

4. What was Jesus' response to the Pharisees' accusation that He broke the Jewish law?

5. The enemies of Christ attacked Him on four different fronts. Discuss briefly each of the four accusations.

The Gospel

Chapter Five

Jesus lives His life through the believer as the Holy Spirit indwells the believer. The saint is called first to a love relationship with Him, and the fruit of that love will be the true works for which the church is to be known. Service that flows out of love is the real service according to the Spirit.

Come to Me

"Come to Me, all you who labor and are heavy laden, and I will give you rest. Take My yoke upon you and learn from Me, for I am gentle and lowly in heart, and you will find rest for your souls. For My yoke is easy and My burden is light." (Matt. 11:28-30)

These well known words of Jesus were spoken to the multitudes that had been hearing Him preach. As He looked out on the masses of people, He saw weariness and heaviness, not the joy that should typify the people of God. Numerous times the scripture likens the people of God to sheep. Sheep are not beasts of burden; they were not created to carry weights. Sheep would simply crumble and break down under such stress. Yet this is what Jesus was seeing as He observed the multitudes.

To those that labor and are heavy laden, the Lord extends the invitation to come to Him and He will give them rest. There is only one other place in scripture where the Lord gives an invitation with the words "Come to Me." That is found in John 7:37-

39, and the message there is very similar. There He spoke of the Holy Spirit that would be given after Jesus was glorified. According to Is. 28:11-12, as interpreted by Paul in 1 Cor. 14:21, the life of "rest" is that which is lived in the Spirit. This agrees entirely with the message of Jesus in this portion of the gospel of Matthew.

The people to whom Jesus ministered were fatigued and failing of strength; they had become worn out. The phrase "heavy laden" is similar to the idea of cargo being loaded on a large boat for transport overseas. Under such pressure, all joy had vanished, and praise was not found upon the lips of the people of God.

What then, could be the source of this depressive lifestyle? What had brought such desolation on the nation? Why did both John the Baptist and Jesus find such a spiritual vacuum in the land where their messages of the kingdom of heaven attracted people by the thousands? What had loaded them down? What had been imposed on the ordinary person that had drained him of joy in life?

Various other writers of the New Testament confirmed the answer provided by Matthew. That which had drained the life of the nation was none other than the erroneous interpretations the Pharisees had forced on the Law of Moses. This is one of the themes that Matthew deals with continuously. When harshly denouncing the Pharisees, Jesus sternly declared that the scribes and the Pharisees sat in Moses' seat and, by their faulty interpretation, bound heavy burdens on the nation that were grievous to be borne (Matt. 23:1-4). The scribes and Pharisees, with no comprehension of the nature of God or His love, no concept of the intent of the Law, had missed its point entirely. The Law, under their handling, had degenerated into a system of outward works and observances and had actually been twisted to serve the Pharisees' own lusts.

Luke confirmed this in his gospel. The lawyers (interpreters of the Law) had laden men with burdens grievous to be borne and had taken away the key of knowledge (Luke 11:46,52). Paul spoke of the Judaizers' legalism as a yoke of bondage (Gal. 5:1) and Peter referred to the same legalizing teachings as a yoke that neither his nor their fathers' generations could bear (Acts 15:10). All the writers use the same descriptive words found in the passage from Matthew: heavy laden, burden, and yoke. Legalism was the culprit.

The Law, as intended by God, is to be written on the tables of men's hearts as an expression of love. This is to show how love behaves. The scribes and Pharisees simply turned it into a system of outward rules, and holiness became a matter of washing hands, or the traveling distance during the Sabbath. This legalism, void of inner reality with no knowledge of God, exacted demands on the natural efforts of man to obtain holiness; but the gospel clearly states that achieving holiness in this manner is an impossibility for man. No wonder the masses had become worn out!

Salvation is not attainable by human efforts. Sanctification is not the result of human endeavors. All is by grace. Grace is not only "unmerited favor" but also "operational power." The Holy Spirit changes and influences the heart so that a man's interior life is altered and reoriented. Then, this work of the Holy Spirit is demonstrated by outward change of behavior.

To the multitudes that were laboring under this false premise, Jesus made this offer. He will give them rest by having faith in Him! Man was not created to carry the kinds of burdens that the Pharisees imposed; man was created to be filled with the presence of God. Adam was created on the sixth day; the man and the woman were the last to be created in the six days of creation. On the seventh day God rested. Thus Adam's first full day of existence was to enjoy the rest of God! In resting on the seventh day, God filled all creation with Himself and sanctified it (Gen. 2:2-3). It is the presence of God that makes holy. It is from this "rest" that man fell, and it is this "rest" which is restored at salvation. This rest is obtained by faith in Christ; it is not attained through a system of works. This is the truth brought out by the writer of Hebrews, in which the definition of "rest" is given as "ceasing from one's own works" (Heb. 4:1-11; especially verse 10).

There have been numerous testimonies of people coming to Christ, and when their burdens were cast on Him, the Holy Spirit filled their vacant hearts with great peace. Indeed, they were given "rest." Unfortunately though, this life of rest could not be maintained. Soon the sincere believer in Christ finds himself under the same load as before. Often this is the result of a renewed consecration to please the Lord in all things, which should be the case, but not from the same false premise as before. It is a failure to see the sufficiency of Christ for all things in life, and an effort is made once again to please the Lord by works of the flesh.

Thus the teaching of Christ progresses from the believer being "given" rest to "finding" rest. Abiding in rest is the fruit of "learning of Him." Christ Himself is the Christian life. God does not give the believer different virtues, but He gives His own Son, in whom are all things. This is the overwhelming statement of scripture, and it is reflected in verses such as:

> *"I have been crucified with Christ; it is no longer I who live, but **Christ lives in me**; and the life which I now live*

in the flesh I live by faith in the Son of God, who loved me and gave Himself for me." (Gal. 2:20)

*"**For to me, to live is Christ**, and to die is gain."* (Phil. 1:21)

*"Blessed be the God and Father of our Lord Jesus Christ, who has **blessed us with every spiritual blessing in the heavenly places in Christ.**"* (Eph. 1:3)

Therefore, the duty of the believer is to "learn of Christ." Jesus lives His life through the believer as the Holy Spirit indwells the believer. The saint is called first to a love relationship with Him, and the fruit of that love will be the true works for which the church is to be known. Service that flows out of love is the real service according to the Spirit.

When the Holy Spirit led Jesus into the wilderness, Christ encountered temptation from the evil one. One of the temptations involved Satan offering to Jesus all the kingdoms of the world if He would but bow down to worship him. In response, Jesus quoted Deut. 6:13 as the guiding principle by which He would live His life (Matt. 4:8-10). Indeed, within this quote is the truth concerning worship and service. The verse simply states:

*"Then Jesus said to him, 'Away with you, Satan! For it is written, **You shall worship the Lord your God, and Him only you shall serve.**' "* (Matt. 4:10)

From this, it is easily observed that service flows directly out of worship. In other words, a person serves what he loves. When someone loves something, no obstacle is too great and no expense is too much for the sake of what is loved. When loves rules the heart, no command is grievous. All is done with pleasure. The gospel puts no credence in works as a factor by which

God justifies a believer, but it does indeed demonstrate that works will follow where the heart has been changed. The laws of God are written on it to teach it how to love God and neighbor (Eph. 2:8-10; Titus 1:16; 2:7,14; 3:1,8,14).

Thus the great imperative is to worship Christ. To know Him is to worship Him. Love for Him will unconsciously betray itself in words and deeds that reflect God's character. This is the life of the Spirit.

This is the yoke Jesus said the believer is to take. "To come under a yoke" is another way of saying "to submit to a teaching." Following the commands of Jesus is not difficult to a heart that adores Him. It is natural, not hard.

Jesus was not inclined to bring attention to any of His attributes. However, on this occasion, the listening crowds are to take note of His meekness and lowliness of heart. Rest is available to those of like nature. A proud individual cannot find rest, for he must perform and work out of his own resources. Having to prove a point, or to be noticed, he must resort to self-effort, thus robbing him of the rest that is enjoyed in God.

Thus by worshiping God, by loving the Lord, one is set free from endeavoring by self-effort to please Him. The soul is at rest. Often, scripture uses the term "soul" as opposed to "spirit" when the human self is in view, as it is in this case. Life in the Spirit, which is the rest for the believer, simply follows the expression of love. The Christian life is not duty, but joy. Love has the amazing ability to empower and give life. It energizes and gives strength for whatever task it seeks to accomplish.

Thus Jesus concluded His famous saying stating that His yoke is easy, and His burden is light. The word "easy" is otherwise translated "kind" or "gentle" in other portions of scripture. The command of Jesus is not grievous. A new heart dominated by the love of God, returning love for love, will indeed find that His burden is light.

Thought Questions

1. The people to whom Jesus ministered were fatigued and depressed. What was responsible for this condition?

2. Salvation is not attainable by human efforts. Explain.

3. Often, after the Holy Spirit has filled the heart of a new believer with peace, this rest cannot be maintained. What do you think is the reason for this?

4. Jesus said, *"You shall worship the Lord your God, and Him only shall you serve."* Do you believe the placing of the words "worship" and "serve" could be reversed without changing the meaning of the quoted statement?

Chapter Six

The Rich Young Ruler
Matthew 19:16-22

Unconsciously, most believers think of this story as a composite of the three synoptic accounts (Matthew, Mark, Luke). All three say this man was rich, for that is the point of the story, but only Matthew mentions he was young, and only Luke informs the reader that he was a ruler of a synagogue.

As this story takes place, the final months of the life of Jesus are upon Him. Because the Galileans are unhappy with Him for His decision not to march down to Jerusalem to be their worldly king, Jesus takes a detour around that area and spends some time in Peraea, the land east of the Jordan River, before going to Jerusalem in Judea. This is a longer but safer route for Jesus to travel, and it is the site where the events of this story occur. There He teaches many of His famous parables that only Luke records, such as sitting in the chief rooms, the great supper, the lost coins, the prodigal son, the unjust steward, and the rich man and Lazarus. Peraea is the home of this rich young ruler, and the story unfolds as Jesus is leaving the area:

> *"Now behold, one came and said to Him, 'Good Teacher, what good thing shall I do that I may have eternal life?' So He said to him, 'Why do you call Me good? No one is good but One, that is, God.* **But if you want to enter into life, keep the commandments.'** *He said to him, 'Which ones?' Jesus said, 'You shall not murder,' 'You shall not commit adultery,' 'You shall not steal,' ' You shall not bear false witness,' 'Honor your father and your mother,' and, 'You shall love your neighbor as yourself.' "* (Matt. 19:16-19)

Note the character of this young man: he is earnest; he has the right desires; he has perfect aim. His testimony is that he is blameless as touching the law (he understands the teaching of the scribes and Pharisees). His legal blamelessness is recognized in that while yet a youth, he was made ruler of a synagogue. He has cravings for something higher than that which he presently enjoys; he was unspoiled by the world in his youth. He longs for a higher life (eternal life), the life God lives, that which is characteristic of God. Indeed, he desires to be a son of the age to come. (His is not just a request to go to heaven and live forever!) He does not come to entrap Jesus as the scribes and Pharisees so often do. He does not seek personal advantage as the five thousand who ate bread in the wilderness; he is not there out of mere curiosity; he is as sincere as he is zealous. For these reasons, Jesus, who sees into the very heart of man, loves him (Mark 10:21). Jesus speaks no harsh words to him and shows him love, mercy, and pity.

After blessing little children, Jesus begins His departure from Peraea. The rich young ruler heard of Jesus and His teachings, but has not yet met Him. Perhaps his Jewish prejudices have hindered him from becoming a disciple, but Jesus appears as a good man, a teacher who perhaps could help him, for he senses something lacking in his own experience. Perhaps this rabbi (Jesus) could point out what he needs. However, Jesus is leaving the area and there is no time to lose. Overcoming his biases, the rich young ruler runs to Jesus and falls at His feet in reverence, as a student before his master and teacher (Mark 10:17). Matthew describes the same situation in Matt. 19:16-19.

Matthew's use of the word 'behold" shows that this is sudden and unexpected (Matt. 19:16). Perhaps the young man's question concerning eternal life comes from hearing about the teaching of Jesus. This young ruler's honest desire for God greatly exceeds that of the scribes and Pharisees of his day! However, his concept of true spiritual life still misses the mark.

He approaches Jesus with the title "Good Teacher." This is not a recognition of His deity, but a supposition that Jesus has "arrived" at this stage of goodness by some discipline or process. What did Jesus do to arrive at this stage of spiritual development? That is the question being asked. It is for this reason that Jesus refuses the title, pointing out that only God is good. Goodness can only be received from God; it is not achieved by a series of acts one undertakes.

The question "What shall I do...?" reflects the "works" or "religious and legalistic mentality" teaching of the scribes and Pharisees. Obviously, the young man believes that spiritual life is attained through rules and regulations. It is a common question between rabbinical teachers and students. Various answers could be given, such as: prayers, reading the Psalms, or giving honor to the aged. Jesus shows this whole approach is wrong. This rich young man shows some self-confidence that he could do whatever it takes. He thinks he is capable, for he has already become a ruler of the synagogue. Most likely, he perceives himself as

approaching goodness because of his own merits and achieve-
ments.

The Lord's answer shows a certain severity. His response is
simply, "Keep the commandments." Notice that Jesus does not
use the phrase "eternal life" but only "life." As will be demonstrated, spiritual fulfillment is found in the ordinary course of
life. This rich young ruler, while keeping the letter of the law
like the Pharisees do, misses its intent and righteousness. He
fails to notice the love of God. It is all too easy to overlook what
makes up true spiritual satisfaction and continue to seek greater
sensational experience in the name of spirituality.

Eager to know what great commandments he must keep to attain
goodness, the man immediately asks, "Which ones?" Jesus had
taught many things in Peraea. To what was Jesus referring?
What sort of commandment does He mean? What great secret
would Jesus divulge in order that he too might arrive? What new
and particular command is he qualified to hear that the ordinary
common person, not developed like he, could not hear?

Jesus' answer is the well-known commands of Moses. Jesus
quotes five of the Ten Commandments that deal with relationships to people. Notice that He quotes them all in order, except
one. He gives the sixth, seventh, eighth, and ninth commandments; then He states the fifth. After giving "negative" (You
shall not) commandments, He gave a "positive" (You shall)
commandment concerning honoring one's parents, which is duty
with a promise of "life" being attached to it (Ex. 20:12; Eph.
6:1-3). He then gives the summary of these commands: *"You
shall love your neighbor as yourself."* It is also important to notice that the tenth commandment concerning covetousness is not
mentioned. Jesus will discuss that later.

It may be possible that Jesus mentions the fifth commandment concerning one's father and mother last because this rich young man is guilty of claiming "Corban" on his wealth. Having dedicated it with a vow, he is free from responsibility toward his parents, since a vow could not be broken. Jesus condemns this practice in no uncertain terms in Matthew 15:1-9.

Surprised, and with a hint of self-satisfaction, the young man claims that he has kept all these commandments from his youth. That he is a ruler of a synagogue while he is still young is proof of his blamelessness before the law. However, he has not kept the Law according to Jesus' interpretation of it; instead, he has kept it according to the perverted principles of the scribes and Pharisees. A twisting of the letter of the Law to serve their purposes is considered legally correct. However, they miss the entire intent of the Law and totally bypass its righteousness, knowing nothing of the love of God that inspired it. The rich young ruler had no inner spiritual reality. Legalism leaves a lack. It cannot fill the void. The law makes nothing perfect (Heb. 7:19).

The perfection the rich man is seeking is the same as achieving goodness in his own sight. Jesus can see into the very mainsprings of his heart. The young man does not know his own heart. The righteousness of the Law as Jesus taught it in Matthew 5 is totally unknown to him. Jesus gives him a test, designed for his need of self-revelation. In essence, it is a test concerning the tenth commandment, "You shall not covet." This is the one commandment Jesus does not quote.

The test reveals the condition of his heart. The "legal" keeping of the letter of the law does not produce the righteousness that satisfies, nor that which is acceptable to God (c.f. Phil. 3:3-9). While the young man could say he "kept" the law as it had been taught by the scribes and Pharisees, he does not know he is void of the righteousness of the Law. This is what produces his "lack."

The command to sell all that he has (Luke 18:22) and give it to the poor unveils the utterly selfish, unrighteous condition of his heart. His definition of "neighbor" is woefully inadequate, as he certainly does not love those in need. He does not understand the Law he claims he has kept from his youth. The Law, as Jesus is now applying it, has convicted him of sin (Rom. 3:20)!

Is it possible that this young man could have joined the disciples? Though he is sincere, his understanding is erroneous. He proves to be unteachable because his heart is conquered by his wealth. Sadly, he could not pass the test.

Because he is very rich, having great possessions, he leaves with sorrow, though not with anger or carelessness. A dark gloom overshadows his face. This is not the answer he expected. The Pharisees teach that wealth is a sign of God's blessing. However, they teach this because inwardly they are covetous (Luke 16:14). They make the Word of God subject to their own desires and interpretation.

Following this, Jesus points out the great danger of riches influencing the heart. The wealth, honor, and prestige of this world harden a man's heart to the things of God and eternity (c.f. 1 Cor. 1:26). Jesus does not say it is impossible for a rich man to enter the kingdom of heaven, but that it is difficult. Fortunately, others have passed this very test that the rich young ruler failed.

When the disciples hear it, they are very perplexed. If it is so hard, salvation is impossible. The response of Jesus says it all. With men it is impossible. As long as the Law remains on tables of stone, the Law is powerless to deliver. But with God all things are possible. The gospel is powerful. It is then a matter of faith and of trusting God to do in one's life what he cannot do himself.

This story reveals several things about the Law, the gospel, and salvation. They are:

1. As in this young man, the Law awakens a desire for God and His righteousness. There is a morality, purity and cleanliness that is of higher order than that which man can produce.
2. Though it awakens a desire for purity, the Law cannot produce it. Strive as one may, there will always be a lack. The harder one pursues righteousness with his own ability, the further away it becomes.
3. The preaching of the Law convicts of sin, as it is discovered that the righteousness God demands and the person desires is not within. The Law reveals the sinfulness of human nature.
4. Salvation is not attainable by human means. God must do in a person that which he cannot do himself.
5. Salvation is not to be limited in meaning to the forgiveness of sins only. It is coming under the yoke of Christ. Salvation is the righteousness of God being engraved on the tables of the heart, producing righteousness in life-style.
6. Salvation involves the removal of whatever has been revealed by the Law that is not in harmony with God. In this case, the heart of the rich young man was covetous and in disharmony with the nature and righteousness of God. Sin must be forsaken in order to have the laws of God written on the tables of the heart. This is repentance. The command to sell all and give it to the poor is a particular command to the rich young ruler. Jesus gives different answers to dif-

ferent people, according to their needs and view-points. Each individual receives prescribed surgery.

7. Spiritual fulfillment is not found necessarily in the spectacular. Signs and wonders are important to the gospel, but they are not the end of it. The end of the gospel is the establishing of righteousness. Jesus defines the righteousness that is eternal as loving God and neighbor. Spiritual satisfaction will be found in the ordinary routines of life; it is present in relationships as the Holy Spirit sheds the love of God abroad in the hearts of men.

Thought Questions

1. Describe the character of the rich young ruler.

2. Why did the rich young ruler want to meet Jesus?

3. What is incorrect about the rich young ruler's understanding of attaining eternal life?

4. What was Jesus' recommendation to him concerning the achieving of eternal life?

5. Explain why the fifth commandment may have been a burden to the rich young ruler.

6. According to Jesus, it is difficult for a rich man to enter the kingdom of heaven. Why is this so hard?

7. Salvation involves the removal of whatever has been revealed by the Law that is not in harmony with God. Comment on this statement.

The Rich Young Ruler

Section III.

Two Kinds of Interpretations

Section III

Chapter Seven

The scribes and Pharisees limited their understanding to purely externals, while Jesus applies the Law to the inward springs of the heart from which all sin proceeds. The position of Jesus, which is the foundation for His interpretation in this present chapter (Matthew 5), is clearly stated in Matthew 15: 18-20.

But I Say to You
Matthew 5:17-48

*"Do not think that I came to destroy the Law or the Prophets. I did not come to destroy but to fulfill. For assuredly, **I say to you, till heaven and earth pass away, one jot or one tittle will by no means pass from the law till all is fulfilled.** Whoever therefore breaks one of the least of these commandments, and teaches men so, shall be called least in the kingdom of heaven; but whoever does and teaches them, he shall be called great in the kingdom of heaven. **For I say to you, that unless your righteousness exceeds the righteousness of the scribes and Pharisees, you will by no means enter the kingdom of heaven."** (Matt. 5:17-20)*

The Law demands the righteousness that Jesus came to fulfill. The teaching and preaching of the gospel should foster the righteousness that the Law requires, for that is the righteousness of God. What is the righteousness of the Law? Of what does righteousness consist?

The above portion of scripture makes it plain that Jesus did not come to do away with the righteousness of the Law. However, he did come to rescue it from the perversion of the scribes and Pharisees. The doctrines of the scribes and Pharisees, according to Jesus, did not reflect the true nature of the Law. In opposing the interpretations of these "doctors of the law," Jesus did not discard the Law itself. Rather, He disentangled it from their perversions and restored to it the correct interpretation. Jesus declared that the true precepts of the Law must be followed to inherit the kingdom of heaven.

In this passage of the "Sermon on the Mount," Jesus does not oppose the teaching of Moses; however, He definitely contests the Pharisees' interpretation of Moses. Six times in this chapter, Jesus states the perverted positions of the leaders of Israel, introducing them with the words 'You have heard that it was said by them of old time' or 'It has been said.' Jesus then gave His own understanding of the Law in each case after introducing His comments with 'But I say to you.' In this manner, Jesus used six commandments of scripture and described how the religious leaders mishandled them. Then, He gave their true meaning and application for life as God intended in the commandments.

In each case, the scribes and Pharisees limited their understanding to purely externals, while Jesus applies the Law to the inward springs of the heart from which all sin proceeds. The position of Jesus, which is the foundation for His interpretation in this present chapter (Matthew 5), is clearly stated in Matthew 15: 18-20. Out of the heart proceed evil thoughts, murders (6th commandment), adulteries and fornication (7th commandment), thefts (8th commandment), false witness (9th commandment) and blasphemies. The source of sin is the heart; the source of the righteousness that pleases God is the renewed heart.

The Question of Murder: The Sixth Commandment, "You Shall Not Kill."

"You have heard that it was said to those of old, 'You shall not murder, and whoever murders will be in danger of judgment.' **But I say to you that whoever is angry with his brother without a cause shall be in danger of the judgment. And whoever says to his brother, 'Raca!' shall be in danger of the council. But whoever says, 'You fool!' shall be in danger of hell fire.** *Therefore if you bring your gift to the altar, and there remember that your brother has something against you, leave your gift there before the altar, and go your way. First be reconciled to your brother, and then come and offer your gift. Agree with your adversary quickly, while you are on the way with him, lest your adversary deliver you to the judge, the judge hand you over to the officer, and you be thrown into prison. Assuredly, I say to you, you will by no means get out of there till you have paid the last penny."* (Matt. 5:21-26)

The Pharisees limit the commandment "You shall not murder" to the outward, physical act of killing. Jesus, however, goes to the source of murder, which is anger. Anger comes out of the same spring as murder. Jesus warns that any person who is capable of anger is capable of murder. This is the awful truth! Most often, it is only the law of the land that prevents many murders from happening. Fear of punishment and losing one's own life represses murder in the heart from expressing itself.

The anger to which Jesus refers in this passage of scripture means that which is long-lived and brooding. It is interesting to note that the words "without a cause" are not in the original Greek. If this phrase is included, some may think it is acceptable to brood in anger if there were a cause. Jesus is warning that

77

anyone who is capable of chronic, brooding anger is capable of physical murder. Anyone harboring this kind of anger may be required go to court for judgment.

"Raca" is a difficult word to translate, because the "tone" of the spoken word may speak more of scorn and contempt than does "fool," the usual translation. To call someone a fool is to throw doubt on another's moral character. Anyone who behaves in such a manner should recognize the need to appear before the council. Anger's intensity can progress from brooding to scorn to contempt. The judgment has also proceeded from a local town council (judgment), to the Sanhedrin in Jerusalem (council), and then to the Gehenna (hell fire)! Gehenna was the refuse area outside Jerusalem that was continually burning, where final judgment was given.

Murder proceeds from a heart that is filled with anger. There are many examples in scripture that demonstrate this truth. John used the example of Cain, who brooded over his own failure and his brother's acceptance by God. John was simply restating the position of Jesus when he said that whoever hates his brother is a murderer (1 John 3:12-15). A new heart that has the love of God written on its tables is the only cure for murder.

Jesus continues to emphasize this to His hearers. A man offering a gift (sacrifice) at an altar is to be clear of offense before others. Suppose a man has stolen another person's sheep. According to the Law of Moses, an appropriate offering was to be brought before the Lord to make atonement. However, the sacrifice was not acceptable if restitution had not been made to the person who had lost the sheep. If it were discovered that no restitution had been made, the sacrifice was void, destroyed, and carried outside the camp as unclean. Clean up offenses with each other! Jesus further illustrates this concept using a case of debt. If one will deal with it quickly, he may avoid charges in court. If the issue is not settled out of court, it will become the judge's responsibility, and out of the offended one's hand. The full penalty of Law will be extracted. In other words, deal with the bitterness, grudges, and anger immediately. Change the course before it goes any further. If left, the judgment of God will be against a murderer, because murder has been committed in the heart before it is physically done. The righteousness that God demands proceeds from a renewed heart! That righteousness goes beyond not committing physical murder to deliverance from anger in the heart that gives birth to murder. It is love written on the tables of the heart that does good even to enemies!

The Question of Adultery: The Seventh Commandment, "You Shall Not Commit Adultery."

"You have heard that it was said to those of old, 'You shall not commit adultery.' **But I say to you that whoever looks at a woman to lust for her has already committed adultery with her in his heart.** *If your right eye causes you to sin, pluck it out and cast it from you; for it is more profitable for you that one of your members perish, than for your whole body to be cast into hell. And if your right hand causes you to sin, cut it off and cast it from you; for it is more profitable for you that one of your members perish, than for your whole body to be cast into hell.* (Matt. 5:27-30)

As was the case regarding murder, the scribes and Pharisees limit the meaning of this commandment to the outward physical act, which they strongly condemned.

Again, the source of adultery is in the heart. By "looking," Jesus refers to a deliberate look with the desire to arouse lust. It meant a deliberate approach to that end. Jesus spoke of adultery as already committed. Adultery is a condition of the heart before it is a physical act.

Jesus uses hyperbole to make His point. A person should take whatever measures necessary to keep the heart clean. If the eye is the gate through which lust enters, get rid of it. If the hand is the culprit, get rid of it too. It is better to go through life maimed than wholly cast into hell at the end. These words of Jesus need to be heard because they underscore the disastrous end and consequences of sin first committed in the heart.

The Question of Divorce

"Furthermore it has been said, 'Whoever divorces his wife, let him give her a certificate of divorce.' ***But I say to you that whoever divorces his wife for any reason except sexual immorality causes her to commit adultery; and whoever marries a woman who is divorced commits adultery."*** (Matt. 5:31-32)

The Pharisees did not tolerate adultery and quickly condemned offenders (c.f. John 8:3-11). Jesus exposes their corrupt hearts as guilty of the very same crime. Moses spoke of the procedure for divorce and remarriage in Deut. 24:1-4. The Pharisees failed to see the love of God in this allowance; instead, they twisted this passage from the Law to serve their own lusts! While they hypocritically hated adultery, they nevertheless served their lusts by pursuing divorce so they could remarry.

Typically, while married to his wife, a Pharisee would tire of her and begin to look on other women with a lustful eye. No longer pleased with his wife and lusting after another, the Pharisee used the divorce allowance of Moses to facilitate his own lust. He would circumvent the charge of adultery by first giving the divorce to his wife and then claiming he was righteous in the sight of the Law

The divorce question is put to Jesus in Matt. 19:3-12. In response, Jesus refers to God's original institution of marriage as recorded in Genesis. What God has joined together, let no man put asunder. The Pharisees thought they had trapped Jesus with this question, for did not Moses give a command for divorce? The Pharisees viewed this passage from Deuteronomy as a "command" to divorce when they felt it convenient.

Jesus corrects them by showing that Moses did not "command" divorce, but "allowed" it. There is a major difference in the meanings of the two words. The sad reality is that sin is part of the human race. If a man hates his wife, what would happen if divorce were not an option? He could be very abusive toward her; indeed, he could murder her to free himself from the marriage. Therefore, because of the hardness of men's hearts, Moses allowed divorce to prevent the greater evil of abuse or murder. In other words, the divorce allowance was given for the sake of love and mercy, for the safety and protection of the woman. The fact is that many people have no intention of doing what is right and will not submit to the will of God. The love of God for the innocent is the motive for giving this allowance in order to save life. Though God hates divorce, He allows it because He hates abuse and murder even more!

It should be noted that other allowances of this sort were made for things that were in themselves abominable, such as polygamy and charging usury. In the case of divorce, the Pharisees separated the allowance from the nature and love of God and used it to serve their own lustful purposes! This is an example of their "righteousness!" By this twisting of the Law of Moses, certain schools of Pharisaism allowed divorce for any cause. Divorce became a simple and all too common procedure. Jesus refuted this by saying that the only reason for divorce in God's eyes is fornication. Sexual immorality is capable of breaking the marriage bond - nothing else does. All difficulties in any marriage can be resolved by adhering to the scripture in the power of the Holy Spirit. This is the righteousness that the law demands and grace delivers!

The Question of Oaths: The Third Commandment, "You Shall Not Take the Name of the Lord in Vain."

"Again you have heard that it was said to those of old, 'You shall not swear falsely, but shall perform your oaths to the Lord.' **But I say to you, do not swear at all: neither by heaven, for it is God's throne; nor by the earth, for it is His footstool; nor by Jerusalem, for it is the city of the great King. Nor shall you swear by your head, because you cannot make one hair white or black. But let your 'Yes' be 'Yes,' and your 'No,' 'No.'** *For whatever is more than these is from the evil one."* (Matt. 5:33-37)

Once again, the scribes and Pharisees twisted the letter of the Law to serve the greed of man, without any regard to the intent of the Law. Their interpretation of the third commandment was not to perjure yourself when using the name of God as your witness (Ex. 20:7; Deut. 6:13). The purpose of this commandment was to insure truth, but the "righteousness" of the scribes and Pharisees twisted this to avoid truthfulness.

What began, perhaps, as a desire to avoid bringing disgrace on the name of the Lord, oath taking became a series of evasive distinctions. Perhaps a man borrowed a sum of money and swore an oath in the name of the Lord that he would repay. However, he found he could not do as he swore, and thus he had taken the name of the Lord in vain. In order to avoid this, it came to be that a person could take an oath in the name of something else and not to use the Lord's name. This way, if failure occurred, it was not the Lord's name that was taken in vain. Out of this a system of binding and unbinding oaths was devised. The whole intention of the third commandment was lost. The hypocrisy of the Pharisees in this area is well illustrated in Matt. 23:16-22, where swearing by the altar was not as binding as swearing by the gold on the altar itself!

When Jesus commanded that the believers should not swear oaths, He was not referring to judicial swearing before magistrates, but in everyday conversation and communication. Oaths were made in the name of heaven, earth, Jerusalem, and even the hairs on one's head. What the Pharisees failed to see was that all oaths were in the name of God anyway, because God cannot be separated from His creation. Their perverted system of what constituted binding and unbinding showed their hypocrisy, and, as in the example of swearing by the gold of the altar as more than swearing by the altar itself, illustrated their greed.

There should be trust between one another in everyday affairs. Taking an oath in daily communication demonstrates that one cannot be trusted. Demanding an oath from another is to discredit his character and reputation. Each proceeds from an evil heart. Again, Jesus has rescued the precepts of Moses by exposing the mishandling of them to suit the perverted lusts of the scribes and Pharisees; He has given the Law its true meaning.

The Question of Justice

*"You have heard that it was said, **'An eye for an eye and a tooth for a tooth.' But I tell you not to resist an evil person.** But whoever slaps you on your right cheek, turn the other to him also. If anyone wants to sue you and take away your tunic, let him have your cloak also. And whoever compels you to go one mile, go with him two. Give to him who asks you, and from him who wants to borrow from you do not turn away."* (Matt. 5:38-42)

The quote concerning the eye and tooth is found three times in the writings of Moses (Ex. 21:23-25; Lev. 24:17-21; Deut. 19:21). The Pharisees completely divorced this saying from its context and God's intent by making it say that God sanctions private revenge - taking the law into one's own hands.

Jesus is not saying that the lawbreakers should go unpunished. That would be contrary to other scriptures. He is teaching that one should not retaliate when he thinks he is being wronged. Like all the laws, the intent of this particular law is governed by the love of God. Because of the presence of hardened hearts, this law was given to protect and give safety to the defenseless of society, such as servants, women and children.

Servants were treated with disrespect, and in anger a master may cause bodily harm to a slave. This law was given to hold sin in check. Its purpose was also to limit revenge. It also needs to be pointed out that this law was for the magistrates to carry out, not the offended party. While the magistrate should judge the guilty party, the offended party must have a clean heart through it all. He is to overcome evil with good. This is the righteousness of God!

The law was to guide magistrates in passing sentence so that a fair judgment was rendered. A hand must not be required for a tooth. A life was not to be given for an eye. This law was not to be misinterpreted to allow private revenge; rather, it was one of mercy on behalf of those who could not defend themselves. For the benefit of society, it is a New Testament principle (Gal. 6:7-8).

To smite someone on the right cheek is to deliver a backhanded blow, a sign of contempt. Rather than be guilty of malice and violence, one is to be willing to submit to further insults. It is better to submit to a repetition of injury than to yield to wrath and sin.

One should not be tied to his possessions either. The coat referred to is a tunic, or inner garment. The poorest of men would have one of these. The cloak is a heavy outer garment that was a robe by day and a blanket by night. A person would possess only one. According to Ex. 22:26-27, this could not be permanently taken from an individual.

Jesus was not condemning the rightful use of courts, but going to court over trifles. Doing so reveals a contentious spirit and a heart for revenge. It is better to rule one's spirit than to protest the loss of one's coat.

Even personal liberties are brought into the discussion. If forced by a Roman soldier to carry his load for a mile, carry it two. Do not retaliate at injustice and inconvenience. Be cheerful and go beyond the command. This is the victory of the inner man, and is the righteousness of God. Instead of standing on personal rights, the righteousness of God serves others.

The Question of Love

"You have heard that it was said, 'You shall love your neighbor and hate your enemy.' **But I say to you, love your enemies, bless those who curse you, do good to those who hate you, and pray for those who despitefully use you and persecute you, that you may be sons of your Father in heaven;** *for He makes His sun rise on the evil and on the good, and sends rain on the just and on the unjust. For if you love those who love you, what reward have you? Do not even the tax collectors do the same? And if you greet your brethren only, what do you do more than others? Do not even the tax collectors do so? Therefore you shall be perfect, just as your Father in heaven is perfect."* (Matt. 5:43-48)

To love one's neighbor is the second great commandment; it sums up the last portion of the Ten Commandments (Matt. 22:34-40). It is found in Lev. 19:18,33-34. The perversion of the scribes and Pharisees is again evident, as they insisted that the command to love was only to one's neighbor. They conveniently adopted a narrow interpretation of the word "neighbor" to mean those who were like themselves. Since the command to love only extended to a neighbor, the Pharisees then justified their hatred for their enemies, since the command said nothing about enemies, but neighbors only!

This is brought out more plainly by the question posed by Jesus on another occasion as recorded in Luke 10:25-37. A lawyer, wishing to justify himself, asked Jesus who was his neighbor. In response, Jesus told the story known as the "Good Samaritan." The truth is, and this is brought out by Moses' use of the term "neighbor" as well, that one's neighbor is anyone with whom one may have contact (See Ex. 11:2; 20:16-17; 23:4-5; Lev.

19:33-34; Prov. 24:17-18; 25:21.) Even one's enemies are his neighbors.

When the command is to love a neighbor as oneself, self-love is not being implied, but rather it is a command to treat others as one would like to be treated.

Acting in this way will verify that the nature of God has been reproduced in the life of the believer. This shows that the believer is indeed a child of his heavenly Father. God's nature is love. Since God sends sun and rain on both the good and the evil, it means nothing if one only loves and responds to those of like nature. Even the despised tax collectors do that! Believers are called to a greater life than that: returning blessings for curses, doing good to those that oppose them, and praying for those who despitefully use and persecute them. This is how God acts, and the saint is to be a child of his Father. This is the standard.

Righteousness is love perfected. This is the end to which Christ pointed as He gave the true understanding of the Laws of Moses. He had been rescuing the Law from the perversions of the scribes and Pharisees by exposing their hypocrisy and self-serving interpretations, their wrangling over the definitions of words, and their lack of any personal knowledge of God or His love. He then placed the Law of Moses in the correct light of the nature and love of God and man. In so doing, Jesus expounded on the true righteousness that is to characterize the life of the believer.

Righteousness is not a set of external rules and regulations that define holiness in and of themselves. Rather, it is love that is the motive and intent of all the commandments. Righteousness is expressed in terms of relationships to both God and man, for

God is love. Love is written on the tables of the heart, and this is the fulfilling (meeting the requirements) of the Law.

Thought Questions

1. Jesus did not desire to do away with the righteousness of the Law; instead, He came to rescue it from the perversions of the scribes and Pharisees by restoring to the Law its correct interpretation. Comment on this concept.

2. (a) What is Jesus' interpretation of *"You shall not kill?"*

   (b) What is Jesus' interpretation of *"You shall not commit adultery?"*

   (c) What is Jesus' interpretation of *"You shall not take the name of the Lord in vain?"*

3. (a) What did Jesus say about *"divorce?"*

   (b) What did Jesus say about *"justice?"*

   (c) What did Jesus say about *"love?"*

But I Say to You

Chapter Eight

> *Jesus made the point that the Law is to be written on the tables of man's heart. This is what the gospel is all about. Grace does not do away with the righteousness of the Law, but it inscribes that righteousness on a new heart! Only when a heart has been changed can a true righteousness that pleases God be lived out.*

Eating with Unwashed Hands
Matthew 15:1-20

Matthew relates the classic story of Jesus and the Pharisees clashing over the eating of bread with unwashed hands. By this time in the history of the gospels, Jesus had a large following in Galilee. Indeed, the miracle of the loaves and fishes feeding a multitude of five thousand men besides women and children had just occurred. To this point, the scribes and Pharisees had been frustrated in all their attempts to discredit Jesus. On this occasion, these religious leaders had been sent from Jerusalem, where the temple was located, to confront Jesus. Their specific task was to find a cause of offense in Him.

Jesus left Capernaum for Bethsaida on a Thursday. (Comparing the story in all the gospels and working back from the Sabbath in which one of the confrontations with the multitudes occurred makes this determination.) Multitudes had gathered around the Master as He healed the sick. It was on that Thursday evening that Jesus miraculously fed the five thousand. Soon, according to John's account of the story, the crowd attempted to take Jesus by force and make Him their king. Rather than submit to such a carnally motivated desire of the crowd, Jesus dismissed them all. He had to strongly demand that His disciples also leave the scene and row across the lake. It is at this time (Thursday night and Friday morning) that a storm arose on the waters, threatening to drown the frustrated disciples (for they were also sympathetic with the crowd's demand that Jesus take on the role of king). This was the night that Jesus walked on the water and invited Peter to do so as well.

Early on Friday morning, the boat landed on the other side, and news of Jesus' presence soon spread. Once again the sick were brought to Him. At this point, the scribes and Pharisees from Jerusalem arrived and accused Jesus of breaking the Law, thus setting up a confrontation in which Jesus accused them of breaking the Law by their own faulty interpretation of it. In Matt. 15:1-9, Jesus reproved them, and then in Matt. 15:10-11, He addressed the multitude to which He had been ministering. As Jesus traveled to Capernaum, further explanation was given in Matt. 15:15-20. After this, the multitude that was previously miraculously fed in the wilderness caught up to Him, at which time Jesus (John 6:22-59) interpreted the miracle to them while teaching in the synagogue on the Sabbath.

It seemed that the anger of the scribes and Pharisees was directed at Jesus because He allowed His disciples and the five thousand He fed the previous day to eat with unwashed hands. To them, this was a breach of the law (their law), making Jesus a sinner.

Matthew assumed his original readers, who were Jews, were familiar with the tradition regarding the washing of hands; therefore, he does not explain it. Mark, who recorded the same story with different readers in mind, does explain the tradition in

Mark 7:2-4. The Jews would not eat without washing their hands, as well as cups, pots, brazen vessels and tables. According to the Mishna (their oral law that acted as a commentary on the written Law), to eat with unwashed hands was a gross carnal defilement, leading to destruction and poverty. A rabbi who didn't observe it would be excommunicated. The washing of hands before eating had become one of the things that distinguished a Jew as unique among other people. It was one of the signs by which a Jew would be known.

To engage in a verse-by-verse study of Matthew 15:1-20 will be advantageous.

"Then the scribes and Pharisees who were from Jerusalem came to Jesus, saying, " (15:1)

The scribes were the theologians and the Pharisees were the pragmatics (having to do with the affairs of a state or community). That they came all the way from Jerusalem emphasized that they were an important delegation. The scribes and Pharisees from Galilee had not been able to successfully accuse Jesus. This delegation was sent to find reason for an accusation against Him to prove he was a sinner. The occasion of eating with unwashed hands provided the format.

"Why do Your disciples transgress the tradition of the elders? For they do no wash their hands when they eat bread." (15:2)

The tradition of the elders was simply their additions to the Law of Moses and their commentary on it. The washing of the hands was a literal application of some of the commands found scattered throughout Leviticus 11. However, they grossly misunderstood the Law and immensely exaggerated it. They conceived an entire method of washing their hands. For instance, they were to lift their hands and let the water run to their wrist. If the food was considered to be "holy" food, they were to immerse their hands and then lift them until the water ran down to their wrists. Then they must pour water a second time with their hands pointed downward to cleanse them from the polluted water. And so it goes! The phrase "eat bread" means to take food. It could possibly in this case have a reference to bread left over from the previous day's miracle (the feeding of the five thousand).

> *"He answered and said to them, 'Why do you also transgress the commandment of God because of your tradition?' "* (15:3)

Jesus immediately challenged the validity of their traditions. Their commentary on Moses must be wrong, for it runs counter to the plain commands of God. The two words "because of" in the phrase "because of your tradition" means "in order to keep, to maintain." When their commentary on the Law came into conflict with Moses, they upheld their tradition and exalted it above Moses!

> *"For God commanded, saying, 'Honor your father and your mother'; and, 'He who curses father or mother, let him be put to death.' "* (15:4)

It is God who gave this command. Mark, in his version of the story, calls it the command of Moses. However, in writing to the Jewish readers, Matthew emphasizes the fact that this is the command of God Himself! It is the Law of God that was being transgressed, not the law of man.

"Honor" means more than obedience and respect. It also includes support and succor, as in aiding them in their old age. This brings a promise of life (Ex. 20:12). Neglect of this command is a curse and is punishable by death (Ex. 21:17; Lev. 20:9).

"But you say, 'Whoever says to his father or mother, "Whatever profit you might have received from me is a gift to God" –'then he need not honor his father or mother.' Thus you have made the commandment of God of no effect by your tradition." (15:5,6)

By using the words "But you say," Jesus is telling them that they are opposed to the revelation that came from God. The Jewish designation for the gift here is the "Corban." It is a vow dedicated to God. The Jews were prone to make vows, many of them rashly. For instance, a person when immersed in a dire situation may promise God many things if he would be delivered out of it. The Pharisee would dedicate his livelihood to God, and according to the rabbis, the vow could not be retracted, even if it meant the poverty of his parents. In other words, a person could avoid his responsibility to his parents simply by making a vow.

Jesus had a reason for using this particular example when approaching the Pharisees at this time. It was the time of the Passover, and many were on their way to Jerusalem. This accounts for the multitudes on both sides of the lake. At this time also, many would be taking offerings to the Lord. By making vows to the Lord, how many would be avoiding their God-given responsibilities?

"Hypocrites! Well did Isaiah prophesy about you, saying," (15:7)

A hypocrite is an actor in a play. He plays a part but is not really the person being portrayed. The Pharisees appeared religious, but they were not God's people reflecting His heart.

"These people draw near to Me with their mouth, And honor Me with their lips, But their heart is far from Me." (15:8)

The worship of the Pharisees was only outward and totally void of any inward reality. They completely missed the significance of passages such as Isaiah 58 and 1 Samuel 16:7.

> *"And in vain they worship Me, Teaching as doctrines the commandments of men."* (15:9)

To worship in vain is worthless and not acceptable to God. The commandments of men stand in contrast to the commandments of God. Their commentary (Mishna) proved not to be revelation from God, but contrary to God. They had perverted the Levitical Law. They missed the point that food does not pollute the soul of man, but disobedience to a positive command does.

> *"When He had called the multitude to Himself, He said to them, 'Hear and understand:' "* (15:10)

Jesus now turned to the multitude and gave them a new concept that would be very hard for their prejudiced minds to accept.

> *"Not what goes into the mouth defiles a man; but what comes out of the mouth, this defiles a man."* (15:11)

Defilement means both intrinsically and morally. To His troubled disciples, Jesus explained more thoroughly what He meant when they also found it hard to interpret what He said.

> *"Then His disciples came and said to Him, 'Do You know that the Pharisees were offended when they heard this saying?' "* (15:12)

Jesus was now talking to His disciples on the way to Capernaum. The disciples had heard what Jesus said, but they were torn between His teaching and that of the Pharisees. They were still somewhat partial to the teaching of the Pharisees and were pressured by others around them. Were they not still feeling some of the disillusionment from the previous day's refusal of Jesus to be made king?

> *"But He answered and said, 'Every plant which My heavenly Father has not planted will be uprooted.'"* (15:13)

The plant referred to is the Pharisee and his teaching. The Pharisaic school of thought must be done away with if one is to receive the truth of the gospel. It is an obstacle to the truth. John the Baptist had earlier stated that the Messiah would "burn up the chaff with unquenchable fire" (Matt. 3:12)!

> *"Let them alone. They are blind leaders of the blind. And if the blind leads the blind, both will fall into a ditch."* (15:14)

The Pharisees will self-destruct. Both the teachers and their adherents are void of truth and understanding. In the end, God will reject them.

> *"Then Peter answered and said to Him, 'Explain this parable to us.'"* (15:15)

Because the parable concerning the defilement of a man was difficult to understand, Peter asked Jesus to explain its meaning.

> *"So Jesus said, 'Are you also still without understanding?'"* (15:16)

Is it possible that after all the teaching, examples, life and miracles of Christ that the minds of the disciples were still governed by the old traditions? Has no true spiritual sense made an impact on their consciences yet? How hard it is for the mind-set to be changed!

> *"Do you not yet understand that whatever enters the mouth goes into the stomach and is eliminated. "* (15:17)

Natural food does not pollute the soul.

> *"But those things which proceed out of the mouth come from the heart, and they defile a man. "* (15:18)

Jesus explained the statement He made earlier in verse 11. That which proceeds out of the mouth reveals the condition of the heart. Matthew has already stated that truth in 12:34-37. Jesus' answer reveals the proper approach to the Law of Moses and how it differs from the interpretations of the Pharisees. The Pharisees were externalists without any thought of inward application. Their actions show this. Compare what Jesus says about them in Matt. 23:23-29. Their definition of righteousness is completely according to the external actions.

> *"For out of the heart proceed evil thoughts, murders, adulteries, fornications, thefts, false witness, blasphemies. "* (15:19)

Jesus offers one of the best clues concerning His method of interpretation and application of the Law. First, the Law is not to be treated as a system of externalisms but as a moral and appealing directive to the heart and conscience. As many passages from the New Testament demonstrate, one of the great purposes of the Law is to expose the sinful condition of the human heart (c.f. Rom. 3:20, as an example). The Law was given to show moral and spiritual value, and it became useless if interpreted externally only.

The accounts of Matthew and Mark vary at this point of the story. Mark itemizes thirteen vices that proceed from the heart (Mark 7:21-23); Matthew mentions seven. However, it is highly significant to see how Matthew comprises his list. In writing to

Jewish readers, he very closely follows the second portion of the Ten Commandments that deals with the believer's relationships with others. Note the order: evil thoughts, murders (6th commandment), adulteries and fornications (7th commandment), thefts (8th commandment), false witness (9th commandment), and blasphemies.

Jesus makes the point that the Law is to be written on the tables of man's heart. This is what the gospel is all about. Grace does not do away with the righteousness of the Law, but it inscribes that righteousness on a new heart! Only when a heart has been changed can a true righteousness that pleases God be lived out. In this manner, scriptures such as Ezek. 36:26-27 are fulfilled.

> *"These are the things which defile a man, but to eat with unwashed hands does not defile a man."* (15:20)

While the Pharisees were purely externalists, with many rules and regulations governing their outward physical lives, there was no inward life touching the heart. Jesus understood the Law as something that is to be written on the new heart of man and worked from within outwardly. Only in this way could one be righteous before God. This was very hard for a prejudiced Jewish mind to accept. Compare such scriptures as Mark 7:18-19; Acts 10:15; 1 Tim. 4:3-5; Rom. 14:14-15; 1 Cor. 8:8. The Mosaic distinction of meats was not instituted for its own sake but to teach the difference between moral good and evil.

Thought Questions

1. Why was it necessary for scribes and Pharisees from Jerusalem to get involved in the situation described in Matthew 15:1-20?

2. What was the "tradition of the elders?"

3. Give examples of the Pharisees' transgression of the commandments of God.

4. Why did Jesus consider the scribes and the Pharisees "hypocrites?"

5. Discuss more fully Jesus' statement in Matthew 15:11.

6. According to Jesus, what things defile a person? Does this list include eating with unwashed hands? If not, why not?

Chapter Nine

The gulf had widened so much between Jesus and the Pharisees that the synagogue was now referred to as "their" synagogue (Matt. 12:9). Jesus' disagreement with them concerning the Sabbath set them against Him forever (Matt. 12:14). Having blasphemed the Holy Ghost, as a tree with evil fruit, they were condemned (Matt. 12:31-33).

The Two Sabbath Controversies
Matthew 12:1-14

Matthew did not place events in his gospel in chronological order; instead, he used a theological arrangement. Here he joined two controversies concerning the Sabbath day. The first story concerned the Pharisees' accusation against the disciples of Jesus; the second related an allegation against Jesus Himself. These two events were placed immediately after the well-known words of Jesus in Matthew 11:28-30:

> *"Come to Me, all you who labor and are heavy laden, and I will give you rest. Take My yoke upon you and learn from Me, for I am gentle and lowly in heart, and you will find rest for you souls. **For My yoke is easy and My burden is light.**"*

The yoke mentioned in these verses refers to submission to a teacher. In contrast to the Pharisees' demands, Jesus declares that His yoke is easy. Matthew, in these two stories, demonstrates the veracity of Jesus' statement.

This chapter is a turning point in Matthew's gospel. The gulf has widened so much between Jesus and the Pharisees that the synagogue is now referred to as "their" synagogue (Matt. 12:9). Jesus' disagreement with them concerning the Sabbath sets them against Him forever (Matt. 12:14). Having blasphemed the Holy Ghost, as a tree with evil fruit, they are condemned:

"Therefore I say to you, every sin and blasphemy will be forgiven men, but the blasphemy against the Spirit will not be forgiven men. Anyone who speaks a word against the Son of Man, it will be forgiven him; **but whoever speaks against the Holy spirit, it will not be forgiven him, either in this age or in the age to come.** *Either make the tree good and its fruit good, or else make the tree bad and its fruit bad; for a tree is known by its fruit."* (Matt. 12:31-33)

God would turn to the Gentiles with the gospel, and Gentiles would rise up in judgment against them (Matt. 12:38-42). It is not the natural descendants of Abraham that can claim to be sons of God, but those that do the will of the Father that is in heaven (Matt. 12:50). In Chapter thirteen, Jesus refuses to speak to them plainly, using parables instead so that they cannot understand his statements. To this point, Jesus had been occupied primarily with preaching the kingdom of heaven and healing the body and soul. Now much controversy with the leaders of Israel will take place.

First Story

"At that time Jesus went through the grainfields on the Sabbath. **And His disciples were hungry, and began to pluck heads of grain and to eat."** (Matt. 12:1)

102

When Luke tells the same stories (Luke 6:1-11), he refers to this Sabbath as the "second" Sabbath. This is a common Jewish term that means the first Sabbath after the second day. The second day refers to the day in which the wave omer is offered at the feast of the Passover. The fifty days of Passover are reckoned from this day. This will be the second Passover of the Lord's ministry. By their actions, the disciples show some progress in understanding. They know that their actions will offend the Pharisees, yet they do it anyway. The Pharisees do indeed condemn this action, and their antagonism becomes much more intense.

The motivation of the disciples is simply that they were hungry. This demonstrates that they were being spied upon.

> *"And when the Pharisees saw it, they said to Him,* **'Look, Your disciples are doing what is not lawful to do on the Sabbath!'** *"* (Matt. 12:2)

The Pharisees continuously plague Jesus, looking for breaches of their law that will permit them to call Jesus a sinner. They attempt to point out to Jesus that His disciples are breaking the law. Hasn't Jesus noticed? Look Jesus! At this very moment they are caught in the very act of transgression!

Based on the Pharisaic tradition and interpretation of the Law, the disciples are accused of secondary violations of the fourth commandment regarding keeping the Sabbath holy. According to Deuteronomy 23:25, their actions are permissible when in another man's field, but that is not the question here. The debate centers on the fact that this took place on the Sabbath day. The disciples are accused of two offenses, both sowing and reaping. This is reckoned as two sins and will require two sin offerings.

"But He said to them, 'Have you not read what David did when he was hungry, he and those who were with him: **how he entered the house of God and ate the showbread which was not lawful for him to eat, nor for those who were with him, but only for the priests?** *Or have you not read in the law that on the Sabbath the priests in the temple profane the Sabbath, and are blameless?' "* (Matt. 12:3-5)

Jesus answers their faulty position by appealing to the Prophets and the Law. By using the story of David, He demonstrates the higher principle of saving life as opposed to the letter of the Law for its own sake. It should be obvious that the very commands of God demanding the priests to minister on the Sabbath must breach the Pharisees' definition of work, and yet they are held as blameless.

"Yet I say to you that **in this place there is One greater than the temple.** *"* (Matt. 12:6)

Here Jesus claims His deity. If God permitted David and the priests to violate the holy food and the Sabbath for a lesser temple, then certainly the disciples are clear of guilt for eating in the service of a greater temple!

"But if you had known what this means, **'I desire mercy and not sacrifice,'** *you would not have condemned the guiltless. "* (Matt. 12:7)

Jesus quotes from Hosea 6:6. The letter of the Law must be understood in relation to the heart of God, so that in obeying the Law, God is being served. Jesus had already quoted the same scripture in Matthew 9:13, but the scribes and Pharisees had not heeded those words. Religion has a tendency to condemn by its interpretation that which is not guilty before God.

"For the Son of Man is **Lord even of the Sabbath."** (Matt. 12:8)

Mark 2:27 states that the Sabbath is intended for the delight, enjoyment, profit, welfare and happiness of man. The Pharisees, in pursuing the letter of the Law without any knowledge of God Himself, obviously missed the point and instead made man for the Sabbath, which made the Sabbath a terrible burden for man.

Second Story

"Now when He had departed from there, **He went into their synagogue.** *"* (Matt. 12:9)

Matthew refers to the synagogue as "their" synagogue. It does not belong to Jesus, nor is He identified with it. It is not His Father's house; it belongs to the Pharisees. They dominate it with their traditions and interpretations of the Law. The separation between Jesus and the leaders of Israel is widening.

"And behold, there was a man who had a withered hand. And they asked Him, saying, **'Is it lawful to heal on the Sabbath?'** *- that they might accuse Him."* (Matt. 12:10)

The man was probably planted there by the Pharisees to set up an occasion for Jesus to heal on the Sabbath day. Healing is considered work, and according to them, it should wait until the next day. Therefore, Jesus will be violating the fourth commandment by healing on the Sabbath day and will be guilty of breaking the law. Thus, He can be condemned a sinner!

"Then He said to them, **'What man is there among you who has one sheep, and it falls into a pit on the Sabbath, will not lay hold of it and lift it out?** *Of how much*

more value then is a man than a sheep? Therefore it is lawful to do good on the Sabbath.' " (Matt. 12:11-12)

Jesus simply shows how hypocritical the Pharisees are. In the name of saving their own herds, they themselves will save life on the Sabbath day and not consider it work. How much more then for the sake of men? The argument speaks for itself.

"Then He said to the man, 'Stretch out your hand.' And he stretched it out, and it was restored as whole as the other." (Matt. 12:13)

The man is healed without Jesus performing any work.

"Then the Pharisees went out and plotted against Him, how they might destroy Him." (Matt. 12:14)

Now, the separation is complete. Israel has rejected Jesus, and Jesus has rejected Israel. In Matthew's gospel, this chapter is the turning point. In chapter thirteen, Jesus begins to speak in parables for the express purpose of hiding His message from the hypocritical leaders.

The Pharisees fail to see that the heart of God is to save life. Their handling of the Law destroys the very intent of the Law!

The Pharisees had led the nation to oppose the Messiah. The nation would then be led to judgment, a judgment more severe than that of the godless heathens throughout history.

Thought Questions

1. "Religion has a tendency to condemn by its interpretation that which is not guilty before God." Comment on this statement.

2. *"The Sabbath was made for man, and not man for the Sabbath. Therefore the Son of Man is also Lord of the Sabbath."* What direction do you think Jesus is giving you regarding the Sabbath day?

3. What is the major consequence of the confrontation between Jesus and the Pharisees concerning the Sabbath? Has this disagreement provided any positive effect on your life?

4. Jesus declared, *"For My yoke is easy and My burden is light."* To whom was He speaking and what was His message?

The Two Sabbath Controversies

Chapter Ten

> *The kingdom of heaven is a spiritual reality now. It may be defined as learning righteousness and grace progressively under the authority of God. The kingdom has been inaugurated; it shall be consummated at the Lord's return. It carries with it a future reward at the second coming of Christ.*

If the Mighty Works Which Were Done in You

"Then He began to rebuke the cities in which most of His mighty works had been done, because they did not repent: **'Woe to you, Chorazin! Woe to you Bethsaida! For if the mighty works which were done in you had been done in Tyre and Sidon, they would have repented long ago in sackcloth and ashes.** *But I say to you, it will be more tolerable for Tyre and Sidon in the day of judgment than for you. And you,* **Capernaum, who are exalted to heaven, will be brought down to Hades; for if the mighty works which were done in you had been done in Sodom, it would have remained until this day.** *But I say to you that it shall be more tolerable for the land of Sodom in the day of judgment than for you."* (Matt. 11:20-24)

Matthew does not place these words in the chronological order of Jesus' ministry; he inserts them to make a theological point.

Matthew records His harsh rebuke in connection with the rejection of John the Baptist. Historically, this passage belongs to the time when Jesus sent out the seventy, after His Galilean ministry was finished (Luke 10:1-16).

These words express pity as well as righteous anger. The word "woe" has the connotation of "alas," an exclamation expressive of sorrow, grief, pity or concern. Jesus is not reacting because He had been insulted; however, the reaction does express His broken heart, because the offer of that which is most precious had been rejected.

To best understand this saying of Jesus, it would be wise to review the teaching of Matthew concerning salvation, righteousness, repentance, the Law, and the heart of man:

The Law convicts of sin. It reveals the external righteousness of God and unveils man's unrighteousness.

Jesus declares many times that righteousness is not attainable through rules and regulations because man's problem is his heart (Matt. 5:8,28,37; 6:21; 11:29; 12:34,35; 13:15,19; 15:8,18,19; 18:35; 19:8; 22:37; 24:48).

Salvation is having the Laws of God written on the tables of the heart. It is not only the forgiveness of sin, but also it is righteousness becoming a life principle springing out of a new heart (c.f. Rom. 8:4). The definition of grace must include operational power besides unmerited favor, enabling the believer to live out the righteousness that pleases God. That righteousness is the love of God shed abroad in the heart by the Holy Spirit that is given (Rom. 5:5). It is demonstrated as the fruit of the Spirit (Gal. 5:22-23). Conversion is to produce a lifestyle of

110

righteousness. Failure in the development of righteousness signifies an inadequate understanding of salvation.
Salvation is the internalization of the Laws of God (Matt.
19:16-26).

Matthew continuously emphasizes righteousness. It is
the whole tenor of Jesus' ministry (Matt. 3:15). One of
Matthew's motives in writing this epistle is to warn of
"carnal security," that is, believing a gospel that does not
produce righteousness as Jesus defines it. Matthew frequently refers to the righteous, the unrighteous, the just
and the unjust (1:19; 3:15; 5:6,10,20,45; 6:1,33; 9:13;
10:41; 13:17,43,49; 21:32; 23:28,29,35; 25:37,46;
27:19,24). These qualities are mentioned twenty-seven
times.

Repentance is obviously part of the gospel. Unrighteousness, which is revealed by the Law, is to be forsaken. As
in the case of the rich young ruler, the issue that held his
heart captive needs to be broken. This is also what John
the Baptist meant when he said, "Therefore bear fruits
worthy of repentance." (Matt. 3:8). This means different
things for different people, depending on how the unrighteousness manifests itself (Luke 3:10-14). The
preaching of John the Baptist is a message of repentance
(Matt. 3:2,8,11). This is how the way of the Lord is prepared. Jesus preaches the same message (Matt. 4:17).
Repentance is necessary to enter the kingdom of heaven.

The kingdom of heaven is a spiritual reality now. It may
be defined as learning righteousness and grace progressively under the authority of God. The kingdom has been
inaugurated; it shall be consummated at the Lord's return. It carries with it a future reward at the second coming of Christ.

In professing Christianity, there is and will be the false as well as the true. Righteousness, in the end, will determine who is true and who is not (Matt. 13:37-43, 47-50; 22:1-14; 25:1-13,37,46). Matthew mentions wheat and tares, wise and foolish virgins, sheep and goats, good and bad fish, and an ill-clad guest at the banquet. Repentance is the entrance to righteousness. Matthew refers to it often (Matt. 3:2,8,11; 4:17; 9:13; 11:20,21; 12:41; 21:29,32).

The aim of preaching the gospel is to bring repentance. This is the initial work of the Holy Spirit in one's life (John 16: 7-12). The teaching of Jesus declares that a work of God is successful only if hearts are brought to repentance. Great miracles take place; signs and wonders occur; yet, the hearts of men often remain unchanged. Rather than yielding to God, people "use" the power of God for their own purposes and lusts. The righteousness of the Law is not sought after; consequently, the love of God is not reproduced in the hearts of men.

Chorazin, Bethsaida, and Capernaum failed for this reason. Indeed, this was the sad situation throughout Galilee. Moreover, the entire nation did not yield to God. It chose its own religious interpretations. The signs were not heeded. This is the reason for Jesus' sorrow over what could have been.

Chorazin, a small village close to the lake in Galilee, is mentioned only in this story (Matt. 11:20-24 and Luke 10:1-16). Bethsaida (meaning "fishing town"), also close to the lake of Galilee, was the birthplace of Philip, Peter, and Andrew (John 1:44; 12:21). No miracle in this place is recorded in scripture. Only what was in the scope of the gospel writer's purpose was used in the construction of this narrative. The gospels are theological books, not histories (c.f. John 21:25).

There was another Bethsaida located on the east side of the Jordan River in the land of Gaulonitus. These two Bethsaidas were on opposite sides of the river in different provinces, and some scholars feel that the two were practically the same town divided by a border, the river. Western Bethsaida in Galilee remained a small village, while Herod Philip built eastern Bethsaida into a beautiful city. Though it affected many Galileans, the miraculous feeding of the five thousand took place just outside eastern Bethsaida. (Matthew 14:34 states that the journey by ship across the lake landed them in Gennesaret, which is on the northwest of the lake.) The healing of the blind man who first saw men as trees walking is believed to have occurred in eastern Bethsaida, since Jesus and His disciples had immediate access to the towns of Caesarea Philippi (Mark 8:22-27).

Though Chorazin and Bethsaida are obscure in the scriptural record, the town of Capernaum is well documented. It became the hometown of Jesus after His rejection at Nazareth (Matt. 4:13-16, 9:1; Luke 4:31). Many outstanding miracles occurred there.

The towns of Galilee had been afforded some of the greatest privileges and opportunities ever granted to any place. However, this did not bring repentance, and consequently, they will be held to a greater accountability in the day of judgment. It would be more tolerable for Sodom, a longtime byword for iniquity (Gen. 13:13; 19:1-29; Is. 1:9, 3:9), than for the Galilean towns. The sins of Chorazin and Bethsaida were very wicked indeed. The inhabitants of Sodom would have repented if they had received the same light, but they perished in the days of Abraham! Neither would Tyre and Sidon, Phoenician sea-faring cities in existence as the Lord spoke, be held to the same degree of accountability! This is a remarkable statement, especially when the denunciations spoken against these cities (Sodom, Tyre, and Sidon) by the prophets are considered (c.f. Is. 23:1-18; Jer.

25:15,22; 47:4; Ezek. 26-28). Yet the Galilean towns would be held more accountable. Tyre and Sidon were similar to Bethsaida and Chorazin commercially, but the Galilean towns had likely condemned the Phoenician towns for their idolatry and unrestrained behavior. The difference between them is that Tyre would have repented in sackcloth and ashes (c.f. Ezek. 26:16)! Capernaum had become proud, and it desired to be exalted to heaven (c.f. Is. 14:13-15).

Even the Ninevites repented at the preaching of Jonah, but the people of Galilee had not repented at the preaching of the One greater than Jonah (Matt. 12:41)!

The privileges and opportunities of Capernaum were powerful and plentiful, as the following chart shows. All of these miracles and events occurred in and around Capernaum, and are listed in chronological order:

	Matthew	Mark	Luke	John
AD 27				
First visit and stay				2:12
Nobleman from Capernaum				4:46-54
Jesus' hometown	4:13-16		4:23,31	
Demoniac on Sabbath		1:21-28	4:31-37	
Peter's mother-in-law, multitudes	8:14-17	1:29-34	4:38-41	
Sick of palsy through roof	9:1-8	2:1-12	5:17-26	
Matthew's call & reception	9:9-13	2:13-17	5:27-32	
AD 28				
12 selected after night of prayer	10:1-4	3:13-19	6:12-16	
Sermon on Mount	5 - 7		6:20-49	
Centurion's servant healed	8:5-13		7:1-10	
Sinful woman washes Jesus' feet			7:36-50	
Accused of blasphemy, ask sign	12:22-45	3:22-30	11:14-26,29-36	
Family seeks audience	12:46-50	3:31-35	8:19-21	
Jairus, woman with issue of blood	9:18-26	5:21-43	8:41-56	

Two blind men	9:27-31			
Demons causing muteness	9:32-34			

AD 29

Feeding of five thousand	14:13-21	6:33-44	9:11-17	6:4-14
Dispute with five thousand				6:22-71

(With this, the recorded ministry of Jesus in Galilee is finished. The events that follow are noteworthy for consideration as well.)

Syro-Phoenician woman's daughter	15:21-28	7:24-30	
Blind man sees men as trees		8:22-26	
Should Jesus pay taxes?	17:24-27		
Who is the greatest?	18:1-6	9:33-35	9:46-48
Woe unto thee!	11:20-24		10:1-16

During the ministry of Jesus, some from Tyre and Sidon had sought Him out (Mark 3:8; Luke 6:17)!

Consider the initial joy and excitement in Capernaum, and so it should be. Jesus had made Capernaum His headquarters since the Nazareth rejection (Matt. 4:13-16). After His first miracle in Cana of Galilee, Jesus visited Capernaum for a short time (John 2:12). Then He went to Jerusalem where He performed many miracles not mentioned in detail. Passing through Samaria (the woman at the well), He again went into Galilee where He was received enthusiastically. His fame was spreading for many Galileans had seen miracles in Jerusalem when they attended the Passover there (John 4:43-45). While in Cana again, a nobleman from Capernaum sought Him out and requested healing for his sick son. Though the boy was at home in Capernaum, a considerable distance from Cana, Jesus restored him to health. Jesus started to teach in the synagogues, and came to Nazareth where He was rejected and expelled from the city (Luke 4:16-31).

Jesus changed residence to Capernaum, and there He cast out an evil spirit from a man in the synagogue (Mark 1:21-28). Such power over demons was new and revolutionary. This was extraordinary, and His fame spread all over Galilee and round about. Jesus retired to Peter's house in Capernaum where Peter's mother-in-law was sick. She was healed and then the whole city was clamoring at the door for Jesus. He healed all that were sick and cast out demons (Matt. 8:14-17).

The next morning, He sought out a solitary place to pray. However, His disciples soon found Him and together they set out on a preaching tour throughout Galilee (Mark 1:35-39). His fame was now such that He could have no privacy (Mark 1:45).

He returned to Capernaum, and as soon as it was known, the crowds again gathered at the door. From every town in Judea and Galilee, He attracted not only the "common" people, but also Pharisees and doctors of the law (Luke 5:17). No one could get through the door because the meetinghouse was so full. Four men brought a friend on a stretcher, but they could not get to Jesus. Therefore, they went through the roof. When the man was healed, everyone was amazed and glorified God, testifying that this had never been done before (Mark 2:1-12).

Matthew the tax collector, who left all to follow Christ, held a reception for his friends and Jesus (Matt. 9:9-13). After a night of prayer on a mountain outside Capernaum, He chose His twelve disciples and preached the famous "Sermon on the Mount."

At Capernaum, a Roman centurion interceding for his beloved servant besought his healing from Jesus. With only a word from the Master, the paralyzed servant was restored to health (Matt. 8:5-13). While having dinner at Simon the Pharisee's house, a woman of the streets washed Jesus' feet (Luke 7:36-50).

As Jesus entered Capernaum again, crowds gathered around Jesus for healing and miracles. He met Jairus interceding for his very ill daughter. On route to Jairus' house, He healed a woman who had an issue of blood (Matt. 9:18-26). Around Capernaum, the blind were healed (Matt. 9:27-31), a miracle not recorded in the Old Testament. Demons were cast out (Matt. 9:32-34). Finally, five thousand were fed supernaturally just outside eastern Bethsaida (Matt. 14:13-21). Many Galileans were present. Surely the greatest privileges ever on earth were granted to the town of Capernaum and the surrounding area.

In Capernaum, Jesus found empathy: thankfulness for His blessings, confidence in His healing power, spontaneous and great joy. Unlike the people of Nazareth who "were offended at Him" (Matt. 13:58), the inhabitants of this area were enthusiastic about His work.

These are the beginnings of the works of God, but is it revival? Did all this bring about the end that God desired?

God, in His mercy, sent a Savior specifically to His people (Matt. 10:6). Moved with compassion, Jesus ceaselessly ministered to the sick and to the demonized. These same people, however, immersed in religious pride, had developed their own concept of what the Messiah "should" be. While they gladly accepted His gifts, they ultimately rejected His message to which the gifts pointed.

If signs and wonders, mighty works, joy, enthusiasm, and excitement are the end to which God moves, then Jesus should have given glowing reports of the "revival and work" in Capernaum. His hearers should have been filled with wonder and awe. Instead, like He did over Jerusalem later (Matt. 23: 37-39), Jesus wept over them with tearful sorrow and a broken heart, because the extraordinary privileges afforded them (privileges that no other city in the world knew) failed to lead them to an inward change of heart. The hearts of men, except for a few (Matt. 11:25-27), remained unchanged. Rather than yielding to God and being concerned for His honor, glory, and purpose, they wanted to use the power of God to serve their lusts, desires, comforts, and purposes. They wanted nothing to do with a spiritual Messiah; they desired a Deliverer who would only grant carnal comforts.

In time, the astonishment turned into familiarity. The residents of Capernaum began to regard the healing virtue of Christ as something at their disposal, almost as their right. The excitement had passed away. Alas, the ground upon which the seed had been sown was not good ground, but stony ground. Ultimately, they were offended at the message of Jesus (Matt. 13:20-21). Rather than yield their lives to God for the great mercy He had shown them, they remained "unconverted." Obviously, they wanted to "use" the power of God as manifested through Christ to pursue their own purposes (John 6:26-27): to rid Israel of Roman occupation, to provide wealth and luxury, and to exalt themselves to position and prominence.

That was the kind of Messiah they wanted. They obviously did not interpret the mission of Jesus as Jesus Himself did. While they gladly accepted Jesus' gifts, they rejected His message: forgiveness of sins, repentance, and a change in the heart of man. They rejected the spirituality of His mission and the kingdom of heaven, since they wanted a kingdom and a Messiah that would serve their desires. In the end, they were not concerned with God's glory, honor, or purpose.

The last great, recorded miracle that affected the Galileans was the feeding of the five thousand in the desert. The multitude had pressed for Jesus to become a king after their desires. Jesus dismissed both His disciples and the crowd, not giving in to their carnal wishes. Very shortly after, Jesus met with the multitude again in the city of Capernaum and spoke to them of their selfish ways. Consequently, many of them followed Jesus no more

(John 6:22-71). After this, Jesus retired to Phoenicia, into the coasts of Tyre and Sidon. There, Jesus found great faith as the Canaanite woman pleaded for her daughter to whom He granted a miracle (Matt. 15: 21-28). Yes, Tyre and Sidon will be more prepared for the judgment day than Chorazin and Bethsaida.

The only references to Capernaum after this are found in the discussion concerning Jesus' responsibility to pay taxes in the city (Matt; 17:24-27) and an argument about who is the greatest (Matt. 18:1-5). No more miracles in Galilee are mentioned.

Chronologically, the utterance of Jesus in Matt. 11:20-24 occurred at this point. Perhaps, in spite of the great Old Testament prophecies against them, Jesus referred to Tyre and Sidon because He had just found great faith there, something not common in Israel. The statement was made when Jesus was sending out the seventy to Peraea (Luke 10:1-24), the Galilean ministry for all practical purposes being finished at this point.

When is a move of God to be considered successful? Is it not when men's hearts are moved to repentance, when people are awakened to the glory of God, and when they are willing to relinquish their selfish purposes? Revival should make God, not the desires of man, the centre of life. God should be given the preeminence; men should lay down self-will. The righteousness of God is to be written on the tables of fleshly hearts, moving men to love one another. Self is crucified; submissiveness becomes a way of life. The aim of God is accomplished when men declare like John the Baptist announced, "He must increase but I must decrease." (Jn. 3:30).

Excitement will not save. Signs and wonders do not necessarily convert the heart. They may not move men to see the heart of God. For all the privileges they experienced, the people of Galilee were unsympathetic (Matt. 11:16-19).

Their sin was greater than that which doomed Tyre and Sidon. They forgot the responsibilities that came with privileges. Greater light means greater condemnation, if it is not followed. They were indifferent: they neither attacked Jesus nor drove Him from their city, but in the presence of God, they persisted in sin and hardness of heart. Their sin was one of disregard and neglect.

They will accordingly be held accountable at the day of judgment. The judgment is fair, and the sentence is not the same for everyone. There are degrees of damnation for the wicked. Guilt will be measured by the divine influence in their midst – opportunities, knowledge, and privileges granted unto them. Did it bring repentance and conviction? Were the people too busy in their own pursuits to have their lifestyles changed? Is the power and presence of God a convenience, or a call to take up the cross and follow Christ? Will a man "use" the love of God, or be "melted" by it?

These words (Matt. 11:20-24) spoken by Jesus also teach that the wicked dead are still alive. Those destroyed in Sodom are awaiting judgment. Justice is not fully vindicated in this world, but in the world to come. What may appear unfair now will be settled then.

Tyre and Sodom will settle accounts with Chorazin and Bethsaida. The damned of those cities will argue that if great signs had been granted with Ezekiel's preaching, they would have repented, even if only in fear. Therefore, the cities of Galilee, Chorazin, Bethsaida, and especially Capernaum, will receive greater damnation. Even Sodom would have been spared judgment.

The men of Ninevah and the Queen of Sheba will rise up in judgment against this evil generation and condemn it. They repented at the preaching of those of less stature than Christ (Matt.

12:38-45). However, Galilee had heard the preaching of One who is greater than Jonah or Solomon but had not repented. Therefore, their judgment shall be greater.

Matthew's stern warning will not be the final word. In spite of all Jesus had said, there were "babes" who did respond (Matt. 11:25-27). This brought Jesus great joy. It was not the many learned and wise in these towns of Galilee (they were the centres of rabbinical learning) who accepted Christ. Those who responded were the foolish ones in the sight of the world. Those who are not proud or conceited with their own intellectualism and accomplishments will see the Father as the Son reveals Him. These will follow Jesus for His sake, for His glory, honor and praise. Dear reader, are you one of them?

Thought Questions

1. Why did Jesus not give glowing reports of the "revival and works" in Capernaum?

2. What kind of Messiah did the people of Capernaum desire?

3. When should a move of God be considered successful?

4. What did Matthew mean by this statement, "Therefore bear fruit worthy of repentance"?

Section IV.

Discipleship

Section IV

Chapter Eleven

The disciple makes a confession of faith and a "public" commitment to Christ and, consequently, has a mission to the world. He is a learner, one who is on the way by putting into practice what he learns, and by making adjustments in life when new revelation is granted. Seeking the kingdom he will inherit in the Day of Judgment, the disciple relinquishes all other securities and interests to grow in knowledge of the Lord.

What is a Disciple?

*"and do not think to say to yourselves, '**We have Abraham as our father.**' For I say to you that God is able to raise up children to Abraham from these stones."* (Matt. 3:9)

*"Many will say to Me in that day, '**Lord, Lord, have we not prophesied in Your name, cast out demons in Your name, and done many wonders in Your name?**' "* (Matt. 7:22)

*"But he answered and said to the one who told Him, 'Who is my mother and who are my brothers?' And **He stretched out His hand toward His disciples and said, 'Here are My mother and My brothers!'** "* (Matt. 12:48-49)

One of Matthew's motives was to warn the church of his day against any kind of false security that rested upon inherited privileges (Matt. 3:9), charismatic powers (Matt. 7:22), closeness to Jesus (Matt. 12:48-49), and other pleas that may be given.

The terms of discipleship are clearly laid out to Matthew's readers. By the time he wrote his gospel, perhaps thirty years after the ascension of Jesus, an entirely new generation had been born and Matthew sought to impress upon the minds and hearts of this age group the meaning of discipleship.

According to Matthew and the other New Testament writers, the kingdom of heaven is both now and yet to come. In other words, it has been inaugurated but will not be consummated until Christ's return to the earth. After entering the spiritual kingdom now, the disciple of Christ must engage in a progressive development that will be rewarded at the judgment day when the Lord appears in His glory. Presently, there are trials to overcome and the outcomes are still undecided. By gaining victories as they work through trials, disciples prove their loyalty to the Lord.

This is too often forgotten, and assurance is easily assumed by a half-hearted commitment to the righteousness of the Law as Christ interpreted and preached it. For now, a disciple is one who is being perfected, implying incompleteness in the present to be fully realized at the end.

A disciple is one who has entered the kingdom of heaven. Discipleship begins with the call to repentance. That was the first announcement of Jesus as He began to preach (Matt. 4:17). Conversion is likened to the heart of a little child (Matt. 18:1-6). Such a spirit involves a reversal of many adult habitual attitudes. It means a complete change. However, for Matthew, conversion is not just a once-for-all time experience, but it is also an ongoing development where faith gives birth to righteousness demonstrated by doing the will of God, visible by good works. That is made plain in the famous "Sermon on the Mount" (Matt. 5-7). John the Baptist made it abundantly clear to his listeners that fruit was required to prove the presence of repentance (Matt. 3:8).

A disciple is a "follower" of another. Matthew demonstrates this through the lives of the disciples rather than by writing a treatise on the subject. The call to His disciples is to "Follow Me" (Matt. 4:18-22; 9:9). Discipleship is achieved by submitting to His "yoke" and being shaped by His teachings, but it is not accomplished just by knowing them (Matt. 11:30). In Matthew's account, five of the twelve disciples are chosen to demonstrate this: Peter, Andrew, James, John, and Matthew himself. The inclusion of Matthew, the despised tax collector, surely implies that the call to discipleship is for all who will come. Matthew assumed two things for disciples: an understanding of and a response to the call of Jesus, and a hunger for righteousness. The disciples are to learn about the kingdom of heaven. Faith to accomplish the works of Christ will come later.

Throughout the gospel, the disciples are treated as learners. God has revealed spiritual things to "babes" (Matt. 11:25). This revelation is not by human effort, but it is granted by the Father (Matt. 16:17). A disciple is one who "does" the sayings of Jesus (Matt. 7:24-27). To those who have relinquished the hardness of their hearts, becoming good ground for the Word that is sown, an understanding of the secrets of the kingdom of heaven will be given (Matt. 13:10-17). This is a privilege many have desired to possess! The very term "disciple" implies that such a person is a learner.

A disciple is one who hungers for righteousness, as revealed by Christ. Several times Jesus describes this as doing the will of the

Father (Matt. 7:21; 12:50; 21:28-32). The gospel gives the power for living before God in a manner that reveals His own nature reproduced in His children (Matt. 5:45,48). This becomes the standard for the disciple - righteousness written on the tables of the heart. The world and its values do not dictate the behavior and mannerisms of disciples (Matt. 20:25-26).

It may sound strange to some readers, but Matthew insists that present discipleship is a tentative trial stage, with the outcome yet to be confirmed. Many that appear first will be the last when the accounts are settled, and vice versa (Matt. 19:30). Not all who are called will be chosen (Matt. 20:16). He insists that believers must endure to the end (Matt. 24:13). Indeed, there must be a hungering and thirsting after righteousness (Matt. 5:6).

Not all disciples were treated with equal privileges. Some were rewarded with more intimacy than others. Peter, Andrew, James, John, and Matthew were introduced in this gospel by an account of their personal call to follow Jesus. Three of these, Peter, James and John, emerged as specially privileged, accompanying Jesus at the transfiguration (Matt. 17:1-2) and in the garden of Gethsemane (Matt 26:37). Of these three, Peter was awarded prominence (Matt. 16:17-19). His eminence was directly due to his heart condition that enabled him to receive revelation from the Father. Thus, it is amply clear that a disciple is one who is "on the way" and that reward is granted accordingly. The call of Jesus is still "Learn from Me" (Matt. 11:29).

Discipleship continues for a believer's entire earthly existence; it is an ongoing, developmental experience. Though the disciples were called as early as the fourth chapter, they needed to be reminded again of the childlike nature of conversion in the eighteenth chapter: "Who then is the greatest in the kingdom of heaven ... (Matt. 18:1-5)?" Jesus emphasizes that only those who possess the humility of a little child are the greatest. Not until the sixteenth chapter did the disciples learn that Christ was to suffer death at the hands of the religious leaders. With this new knowledge granted by the Lord came a new call and commitment to take up the way of the cross (Matt. 16:21-28). This brought forth a call to new decisions and a review of the present life in the light of this new understanding.

Membership in the consummation of the kingdom when Christ returns is not yet bestowed. This may be disturbing to those who have looked for assurance without demonstrating a change of lifestyle. It needs to be emphasized that the scriptures that speak assurance presuppose repentance, sincerity of faith and purpose. Now the believer is to "seek" first the kingdom of God and His righteousness (Matt. 6:33). The Day of Judgment will be the day in which the believer will "inherit" the kingdom (Matt. 25:34).

Matthew puts forth a very disturbing thought: there is a possibility of being repudiated by Jesus in that day. People who have charismatic gifts but do not apply them in following the will of the Father may be distraught on Judgment Day. Jesus will claim that He does not know them (Matt. 7:21-23). If the disciple denies Christ before men, Christ will deny the disciple before God (Matt. 10:33). The evil servant who begins to smite his fellow servant will be cut off unaware and be appointed a portion with the hypocrites (Matt. 24:48-51). The five foolish virgins heard the report, "Assuredly, I say to you, I do not know you." (Matthew 25:12). To those who did not demonstrate love in righteous acts of mercy, the words "Depart from Me, you cursed, into everlasting fire prepared for the devil and his angels" must pierce the heart deeper than can be understood (Matt. 25:41). Matthew leaves no doubt that there is sifting ahead. Every plant that is not planted by the heavenly Father will be rooted up (Matt. 15:13) and there are plenty of tares in the kingdom (Matt. 13:24-30). It is possible that the kingdom of heaven can be taken away from those who think they possess it (Matt. 21:43).

Obviously, the call to discipleship is sharp in Matthew. It is a sharing with Christ in all things: His mission, His authority, and His power (Matt. 10:1-42). This includes rewards for those who share with Christ in all things as well as rejection for those who will not hear the gospel. The disciple is not above his master (Matt. 10:24); consequently, he is not to hide the light under the bushel, but he must shine it before men for all to see a demonstration of good works. The church is to be a city set on a hill, visible to all (Matt. 5:14-16). The disciple makes a confession of faith and a "public" commitment to Christ and, consequently, has a mission to the world. He is a learner, one who is on the way by putting into practice what he learns, and by making adjustments in life when new revelation is granted. Seeking the kingdom he will inherit in the Day of Judgment, the disciple relinquishes all other securities and interests to grow in knowledge of the Lord. He fulfills righteousness in the rule of love, serves while he awaits the hope of the kingdom, and seizes by active faith the power of the risen Christ to serve the world in its diverse needs. This is discipleship as Matthew interpreted it to his and every generation until Christ comes.

Thought Questions

1. *"and do not think to say to yourselves, 'We have Abraham as our father,' For I say to you that God is able to raise up children to Abraham from these stones."* (Matt. 3:9) What declaration is Matthew making in this quote from his gospel?

2. Discipleship begins with the call to repentance. What does this statement mean?

3. Matthew assumed two requirements for discipleship. What are these two necessities?

4. People who have charismatic gifts but do not apply them in following the Father's will for their lives may be distraught on Judgment Day. Analyze this statement carefully. Do you think it may stimulate you to undertake a review of your walk with the Lord? If so, what lifestyle changes might you desire to achieve?

What is a Disciple?

Chapter Twelve

If the need is to carry the lame, blind, dumb, and maimed up the side of the mountain to get to Jesus, so be it (Matt. 15:29-31)! If the church must walk on water to do the will of God, step out of the boat (Matt. 14:28-29)! Faith, as Matthew understood it, is the daring trust that obeys the command of God against all odds and believes God for the results.

Powerless Disciples

"Then the eleven disciples went away into Galilee, to the mountain which Jesus had appointed for them. When they saw Him, they worshiped Him; but some doubted. And Jesus came and spoke to them, saying, 'All authority has been given to Me in heaven and on earth. **Go therefore and make disciples of all the nations, baptizing them in the name of the Father and of the Son and of the Holy Spirit, teaching them to observe all things that I have commanded you;** *and lo, I am with you always, even to the end of the age.'" Amen.* (Matt. 28:16-20)

At the time of Jesus' ascension, some of the disciples doubted. They were unsure of themselves and of Christ's thoughts toward them. Yet, Jesus commanded them to go into the entire world, to all nations, and to make disciples of others.

According to Matthew, they had good reason to doubt; they had failed so many times before! How would they accomplish the task ahead of them now? Matthew's manner of recording the stories included in his gospel is revealing. Each gospel writer picked particular events in the lives of Christ and His disciples and effectively related them to bring out a particular aspect that suited the author's purpose in writing. In the gospel of Matthew, the failure and powerlessness of the disciples are emphasized to a far greater degree than in the other gospels. He declares that the twelve were helpless, fearful, full of failure, and inadequately supplied with resources. Nevertheless, these were the ones that Jesus sent forth into all the nations! What will bring about the necessary changes in these men, permitting them to effectively accomplish their mission to make disciples of all nations? How could their deficiencies be remedied so that they could truly affect society - becoming a light to the world, salt to the earth, and a city set upon a hill (Matt. 5:13-16)?

Matthew tells several stories to emphasize and reveal the disciples' condition. Their failure to accomplish what God had intended to bring to pass was due to nothing but a lack of faith. This is Matthew's diagnosis. The church's inability to cast out demons, to ride out storms, and to minister to the masses of society is due to unbelief, or at best, a half-belief that fails to lay hold of the challenge of the supernatural power of God.

> *"And when they had come to the multitude, a man came to Him, kneeling down to Him and saying, 'Lord, have mercy on my son, for he is an epileptic and suffers severely; for he often falls into the fire and often into the water.* **So I brought him to Your disciples, but they could not cure him.'** *Then Jesus answered and said,* **'O faithless and perverse generation, how long shall I be with you? How long shall I bear with you? Bring him here to Me.'** *And Jesus rebuked the demon, and it came out of him; and the child was cured from that very hour. Then the disciples came to Jesus privately and said, 'Why could we not cast it out?' So Jesus said to them,*

> *'Because of your unbelief; for assuredly, I say to you, if you have faith as a mustard seed, you will say to this mountain, 'Move from here to there,' and it will move; and nothing will be impossible for you.' "* (Matt. 17:14-20)

Though the disciples had been commissioned earlier to cast out demons (Matt. 10:1), they proved inadequate in this instance. Jesus squarely lays the blame on the absence of faith. He emphasizes the smallness of faith required and the fact that literally nothing is impossible to those who have faith. Society is plagued by those bound by demonic powers, whose minds are blinded by the god of this world. The church has been sent to set the captives free. Failure to do so, according to Jesus, is a collapse due to the lack of faith.

> *"But the boat was now in the middle of the sea, tossed by the waves, for the wind was contrary. Now in the fourth watch of the night Jesus went to them, walking on the sea. And when the disciples saw Him walking on the sea, they were troubled, saying, 'It is a ghost!' And they cried out for fear. But immediately Jesus spoke to them, saying, 'Be of good cheer! It is I; do not be afraid.' And Peter answered Him and said, 'Lord, if it is You, command me to come to You on the water.' So He said, 'Come.' And when Peter had come down out of the boat, he walked on the water to go to Jesus. But when he saw that the wind was boisterous, he was afraid; and beginning to sink he cried out, saying, 'Lord, save me!' And immediately Jesus stretched out His hand and caught him, and said to him, 'O you of little faith, why did you doubt?' And when they got into the boat, the wind ceased. Then those who were in the boat came and worshiped Him, saying, 'Truly You are the Son of God.' "* (Matt. 14:24-33)

The failure to continue obeying the Lord's command is again "little faith." Considering the fear of the group, Peter starts well, but he could not finish. Attention is paid to the circumstances rather than the Lord's command, and he begins to sink. The church will go through many storms and obstacles in order to obey the Lord's commission, but it must not be moved by such hindrances, fearlessly walking obediently in the direction that God has given.

> *"Now when He got into a boat, His disciples followed Him. And suddenly a great tempest arose on the sea, so that the boat was covered with the waves. But He was asleep. Then His disciples came to Him and awoke Him, saying, 'Lord, save us! We are perishing!' But He said to them, '**Why are you fearful, O you of little faith?**' Then He arose and rebuked the winds and the sea, and there was a great calm. So the men marveled, saying, 'Who can this be, that even the winds and the sea obey Him?' "* (Matt. 8:23-27)

Apparently, disciples who follow Christ will pass through more than one storm! Following Christ where He goes may cause some to lose their nerve. As the church ministers in the midst of a hostile world, fearful panic may take hold. However, Jesus is not fazed at all. He's at perfect rest and He expects the church to have peace as well. Failure to overcome such paralyzing fear is once again attributed to a half-realized faith that recognizes the power of God but does not accept the challenge of it.

> *"When it was evening, His disciples came to Him, saying, 'This is a deserted place, and the hour is already late. **Send the multitudes away, that they may go into the villages and buy themselves food.**' But Jesus said to them, 'They do not need to go away. **You give them**

> *something to eat.' And they said to Him, 'We have here only five loaves and two fish.' He said, 'Bring them here to Me.' Then He commanded the multitudes to sit down on the grass. And He took the five loaves and the two fish, and looking up to heaven, He blessed and broke and gave the loaves to the disciples; and the disciples gave to the multitudes.* **So they all ate and were filled, and they took up twelve baskets full of the fragments that remained.** *Now those who had eaten were about five thousand men, besides women and children."* (Matt. 14:15-21)

The problems and needs of the world are overwhelming. The church lacks the resources to begin to touch the need. The scope of what God directs the church to do is beyond human ability. Because the disciples very keenly knew their inadequacies and reluctance to do anything about it, they desired to send the people away to meet their own needs. Yet Jesus wanted the disciples to do something about it! They were expected to see every person filled, in spite of their lack of resources. Jesus received what little they could find; He blessed it and returned it to the disciples, who then distributed it among the masses. What a lesson for the church to learn! The provision and power of God is in the command of God. Church, trust Him for all things.

In each of these stories, Matthew emphasizes that a deficiency of faith is the culprit. Matthew alludes to faithlessness on other occasions as well (Matt. 6:30; 16:8). If it is the purpose of these disciples and believers after them to teach all nations, then this half-hearted faith, that recognizes the power of God but does not walk in it, must be removed from their midst.

By contrast, Matthew relates many successes due to the presence of faith in the lives of people who were not disciples. The woman with an issue of blood, in spite of the crowd, pressed through to touch Jesus and received a miracle beyond the medical profession's ability (Matt. 9:20-22). The story of a Roman centurion, who was not an Israeli citizen, provides an outstanding example of what faith should be. Lord, speak the word only! Nothing more is required. Your word is sufficient (Matt. 8:5-13). Disciples, take a lesson from this heathen man! Even Jairus is cast in a good light in the gospel. Though his daughter is dead, he beseeches Jesus to lay His hands upon her that she may live (Matt. 9:18-19, 23-26). Another "non-Israelite" is applauded for her great faith. In spite of resistance, she vigorously beseeches Jesus to deliver her demon-possessed daughter (Matt. 15:21-28). In all these examples, Christ speaks words commending their faith. They received according to their faith. Their faith had saved them!

Matthew purposely emphasizes the role of faith as he records each story. He simply omits details that do not relate to the issue of faith. Sometimes he enlarges the story with details that speak of the marvel of faith.

The church will not know that it needs faith if it cannot satisfactorily define the term. In particular, what does Matthew mean and define by the word "faith?" God used a variety of individuals to write the New Testament. Each one wrote from a particular background and emphasis. Concerning faith, there is a wide variety of emphasis. For instance, faith in the Book of Romans points to a union with Christ in His death and resurrection. It is being "in Christ." The term in the Pastoral Epistles (1 Timothy, 2 Timothy, Titus) has reference to orthodoxy in doctrine, the body of truth that the Christians believe. John used the term to describe insight into divine truth, to know about Jesus. In Luke, it means the acceptance of the gospel. Hebrews speaks of faith as the vision of the unseen. James considers faith without works as mere intellectualism.

The question before the reader is, "What did Matthew mean when he spoke of faith? What is the faith that moves mountains, that conquers fear, that believes nothing is impossible, and that moves well beyond one's own resources? What is this faith by which the church will impact society, both preserving and illuminating it? What is this faith that causes the church to be like a city set upon the hill that cannot be hid?"

Is courage the aspect of faith that Matthew thoroughly emphasizes in both the failure of the disciples and the successes of others? In Matthew, faith is active, visible and audible. It does something; it brings a reaction; it expresses itself in someway; and it is not simply felt or thought. It dares to respond to the Word of God with reaction; it overcomes obstacles or hindrances; it is an overcoming trust that will lay hold of God's will against all odds and circumstances.

Though there is a crowd in the way, the woman with the issue of blood got to Jesus, even if it meant crawling on hands and knees to touch the hem of His garment (Matt. 9:20-22). Reach out a hand! If there are too many people thronging to get into the house where Jesus is, go through the roof (Matt. 9:1-8). If blind and unable to determine one's pathway, follow Jesus and cry after Him (Matt. 9:27-30). If the need is to carry the lame, blind, dumb, and maimed up the side of the mountain to get to Jesus, so be it (Matt. 15:29-31)! If the church must walk on water to do the will of God, step out of the boat (Matt. 14:28-29)! Faith, as Matthew understood it, is the daring trust that obeys the command of God against all odds and believes God for the results.

Yet Matthew defined faith even more clearly. The final question he answered was, "What is faith in?" Surely it is not faith in "faith." Faith is not some magical formula that has power in itself. There is no such scriptural term as the "power of faith." One will search in vain throughout the pages of scripture for such a concept. The faith that Matthew described to the church is faith in Christ Himself. He always makes Christ the focus of his stories while the other gospels writers do not.

Matthew moved Christ to the centre of every story to emphasize that He is the object of faith. For instance, after He healed Peter's mother-in law, Matthew records that she rose up and ministered to Him (Matt. 8:14-15), but Mark's account has her ministering to the others (Mark 1:29-31). The point of the story of Peter's walking on water is to keep one's eyes on Jesus, not on surrounding circumstances (Matt. 14:28-32). Jesus who has the power to heal and to save (Matt. 9:1-8) is the focus of Matthew's story of the paralytic man let down through the roof. As Matthew relates the story of the Gadarene demoniac, he focuses on the centrality of Christ (Matt. 8:28-34). The demons knew His identity. Only a single word from Him sufficed to cast out hordes of demons that were "exceedingly fierce, so that no one could pass that way." The whole city nearby came out to see Jesus. Matthew recorded only those things that pertained to faith in Christ. All the other details about the story must be gleaned from the other gospels.

The faith that makes the church powerful and effectual in the world is a daring faith in Christ, fearlessly moving out at His command, with no regard to hindrances and obstacles. Before His ascension, Jesus had taught that His power and authority were to be shared with His disciples (Matt. 10:1-4). Then He was in His humility; now He is the risen, exalted Christ with all power in heaven and earth given unto Him. He is present in the midst of the church, and is issuing the same command to go into all nations, teaching them to observe all things as He commands, baptizing them in the name of the Father and of the Son and of the Holy Spirit. May the church be filled with the kind of faith that Matthew describes; may the church be cognizant that it is not powerless; and may the church be determined against all odds and circumstances to fulfill the commands of its Savior. Amen!

Thought Questions

1. Each gospel writer picked particular events in the lives of Christ and His disciples and effectively related them to serve his purpose in writing the gospel. What was Matthew's emphasis?

2. What was the reason for this condition?

3. Why was Peter unable to complete his walk on the water?

4. Paralyzing fear is attributed to half-realized faith. Comment on this statement.

5. The power and provision of God is in the command of God. Explain this concept.

6. What is Matthew's definition of faith?

7. The faith that makes the church powerful and effectual in the world is a daring faith in Christ. Comment on this concept.

Section V.

Waiting for the End

Section V

Chapter Thirteen

The forward-looking dimension of the believer's salvation is his hope (Titus 2:13; Rom. 8:23-25). The last of the last days will see the appearing of Christ in all His majesty, the resurrection of the dead, and the judgment seat of Christ! This is the hope that ought to motivate the believer's life and expectations.

Hope Deferred - The End is Not Yet (Pt. I)

*"And you will hear of wars and rumors of wars. See that you are not troubled; for all these things must come to pass, **but the end is not yet.**"* (Matt: 24:6)

Salvation is eschatological (dealing with last or final things). The salvation that was initiated with justification at the first coming of Christ will be consummated with the believer's glorification at His return. The two comings of the Lord inaugurate and close out the redemption story. Having been saved from the penalty of sin (justification), the saint has been granted provision for deliverance from the power of sin (sanctification) and eagerly anticipates the climax of his salvation experience: freedom from the very presence of sin at Christ's appearing (glorification). The kingdom has been inaugurated (Matt. 4:17) and is yet to be consummated (Matt. 25:31). The earnest gives way to the full inheritance; the part loses itself in the whole; the foretaste yields to eternity; and the betrothed come to the wedding day. Day of all days!

The forward-looking dimension of the believer's salvation is his hope (Titus 2:13; Rom. 8:23-25). The last of the last days will see the appearing of Christ in all His majesty, the resurrection of the dead, and the judgment seat of Christ! This is the hope that ought to motivate the believer's life and expectations. God, who has begun a good work in the believer, will continue to do so until the Day of Christ (Phil. 1:6)!

However, Matthew's readers, because of the long delay of Christ's return, lost the initiative to endure to the end. Many could not handle the undesired delay and perhaps even ceased to ask, "Where is His coming?" Their deferred hope destroyed their expectancy. Therefore, Matthew related the words of Jesus to emphasize that a lengthy delay rather than a quick return was to be expected:

> *"... And what will be the sign of Your coming, and **the end of the age?** "* (Matt. 24:3)

> *"... **but the end is not yet.** "* (Matt. 24:6)

> *"But **he who endures to the end shall be saved.** "* (Matt. 24:13)

> *"... and then **the end will come.** "* (Matt. 24:14)

This loss of the future dimension of salvation creates disturbing trends in the Body of Christ. There is a tendency to shift the emphasis from salvation that is to be consummated at Christ's return to a false "triumphalism" for today. (Triumphalism does not allow any trial or weakness in the present. Everything must be a visible outward victory now. Health and wealth are usually emphasized as the true criteria for determining spirituality. It is a doctrine of imminent victory and success.) Without initiative looking to the conclusion of salvation, one is focused to find ul-

timate satisfaction in the here and now. However glorious a believer's experience may be, full satisfaction will not be entered
into until glorification at the resurrection of the body, when all
yearnings and longings will be fully and forever quenched. Until
then, every blessing of God will create a desire for the ultimate
rest to be known in that day. Thus, there will always be on this
side of glory a sense that there must be something more.

This missed perspective of hope thus leads to all sorts of "gim-
micks" or "new keys" or "revelation" to deliver the "something
missing" in the believer's experience. How many fads and new
movements can trace their beginnings to this lost perspective?
How many prophetic schemes have been devised? How many
cults? To meet the need, diversionary spiritual excitements have
replaced hope. Jesus anticipated this and warned the church:

> *"And Jesus answered and said to them:* **'Take heed that
> no one deceives you.** *For many will come in My name,
> saying, 'I am the Christ,' and will deceive many."* (Matt.
> 24:4-5)

> *"Then many false prophets will rise up and* **deceive
> many.** *"* (Matt. 24:11)

> *"Then if anyone says to you, 'Look, here is the Christ!'
> or 'There!' do not believe it. For false christs and false
> prophets will rise and* **show great signs and wonders to
> deceive, if possible, even the elect.** *"* (Matt. 24:23-24)

The absence of anticipation or assurance of future glory also
causes fear and alarm at the state of the world. This will never
fill anyone with joy!

> *"And you will hear of wars and rumors of wars.* **See that
> you are not troubled;** *for all these things must come to*

> *pass, but the end is not yet. For nation will rise against nation, and kingdom against kingdom. And there will be famines, pestilences, and earthquakes in various places. All these are the beginning of sorrows. Then they will deliver you up to tribulation and kill you, and you will be hated by all nations for My name's sake."* (Matt. 24:6-9)

> *"For then there will be great tribulation, such as has not been since the beginning of the world until this time, no, nor ever shall be. And unless those days were shortened, no flesh would be saved;* ***but for the elect's sake those days shall be shortened.***" (Matt. 24:21-22)

Worse yet, without the anticipation of the Lord's return and the sense of reaching a conclusion, the church must settle for what is and be governed by things seen rather than by things unseen. New excitements fade and disillusionment with God sets in. Love grows cold; many fall away; and the conscience becomes blunted:

> *"And then* ***many will be offended,*** *will betray one another, and will hate one another... And because* ***lawlessness will abound, the love of many will grow cold.***" (Matt. 24:10,12)

When the future aspect of salvation is lost from the church's theology, it also loses its initiative for change. Because the mainspring is gone and the future seems empty, the church loses keen and well-founded anticipation. It lacks resilience in adversity, giving way to mere doggedness. Faith loses its power to shape lives; the price of loyalty is too high.

With all the emphasis on the past and present, the fact that the future is "made" is completely absent from the conscience of the church. Living for today leaves no room for preparing against

the day of all days. Future eternal "glories" are traded for temporal momentary "highs" now. As in the days of Noah, concerns
over the present living fill every day:

> *"But as the days of Noah were, so also will the coming
> of the Son of Man be. For as in the days before the flood,*
> ***they were eating and drinking, marrying and giving in***
> ***marriage,*** *until the day that Noah entered the ark, and
> did not know until the flood came and took them all
> away, so also will the coming of the Son of Man be."*
> (Matt. 24:37-39)

This loss of hope's perspective causes one to lose interest in the
kingdom and encourages a self-centred lifestyle. The gifts that
God has given for the kingdom's sake are neglected. If there is
no vision of eternity, why contribute talents against that end? If
there is no climax to which the present salvation is moving,
there is no appreciation of the rewards of that day, nor is there a
consciousness that one's present life and work are preparation
for the last of the last days. There is no knowledge of what to do
in the interim between the inauguration and consummation of
the kingdom of heaven.

Matthew related three parables and a prophetic statement concerning the final judgment to jar his readers free from this loss
of expectancy and its disastrous consequences. He spoke of the
evil servant who abused his stewardship because his lord "de-
lays his coming" (Matt. 24:45-51). There were five foolish virgins who didn't prepare for the bridegroom that "tarried" beyond their expectation (Matt. 25:1-13). There was a servant,
who when his master was gone "for a long time" into a "far
country" buried his talent (Matt. 25:14-30). Then followed a
prophetic word teaching that the reward at the last day is "made"
in the present time (Matt. 25:31-46).

The end was delayed, but it was certain. Had Jesus not emphasized both? The delay was interwoven with the hope. The delay
offered time to prepare for the end. The end was not yet, and the
saint was to endure to the end. Matthew's readers were weary
with waiting; they had almost lost all hope. This loss of future
expectation, according to Matthew, was a large contributing factor to the worldliness, lukewarmness, and unrighteousness found
in the church. To counter this situation, Matthew recalled the
parables of The Absent Goodman, The Ten virgins, The Talents,
and the prophetic warning of The Sheep and the Goats.

The Absent Goodman

*"Who then is a faithful and wise servant, whom his mas-
ter made ruler over his household, to give them food in
due season? Blessed is that servant whom his master,
when he comes, will find so doing. Assuredly, I say to
you that he will make him ruler over all his goods. But if
that evil servant says in his heart, 'My master is delaying
his coming,' and begins to beat his fellow servants, and
to eat and drink with the drunkards, the master of that
servant will come on a day when he is not looking for
him and at an hour that he is not aware of, and will cut
him in two and appoint him his portion with the hypocrites. There shall be weeping and gnashing of teeth."*
(Matt. 24: 45-51)

The evil servant mistakenly thought in his heart that the coming
of his lord is delayed. Since accountability seemed far off, carelessness set in. He developed a more negative attitude toward
others; his personal righteousness declined; and he obviously
lacked self-control. The servant abused his authority and deceived himself into thinking that he could correct his behavior in
time for his lord's return. However, his lord came back unex-

pectedly, and he was cut off along with the hypocrites. The end was sudden.

The Lord requires faithfulness in His service. He asks who will be faithful during the trial of delay. When accountability seems far off or reward appears vague and distant, who will conduct himself in accordance with the end and will feed the flock with appropriate food (c.f. 1 Cor. 4:1-2)? Who is faithful when unsupervised and seeks not a position over other servants? Who, during the delay of the Master, will continue to be a servant and not promote himself to fill the visible power void in the Master's absence? Who will live for eternity rather than for the present and will serve God accordingly (c.f. 1 Pet. 5:1-4)? Is fidelity rare?

The New Testament echoes this theme repeatedly. The Day of the Lord will come unexpectedly, as a thief in the night (1 Thess. 5:2; 2 Pet. 3:10; Rev. 3:3; 16:15). A thief does not announce his arrival; it is a secret. However, knowing that a thief will come is more than sufficient reason for continuous vigilance (Matt. 24:43).

One must be prepared at all times. Each believer will give an account before the judgment seat of Christ (2 Cor. 5:10). This thought filled Paul's mind. He constantly reminded his beloved companion Timothy of his commitment and that he will give an account thereof (1 Tim. 1:12; 4:16; 6:14; 2 Tim. 1:12; 4:18). The church is the Lord's house, and believers are to be faithful servants in that house (Heb. 3:1-6). The Lord of the house is returning. The church is to hold firmly to that which it has been given, to overcome the difficulties it encounters, and to keep God's works unto the end. Thus, it shall be rewarded (Rev. 2:25-28).

The Ten Virgins

"Then the kingdom of heaven shall be likened to ten vir-
gins who took their lamps and went out to meet the
bridegroom. Now five of them were wise, and five were
foolish. Those who were foolish took their lamps and
took no oil with them, but the wise took oil in their ves-
sels with their lamps. But while the bridegroom was de-
layed, they all slumbered and slept. And at midnight a
cry was heard: 'Behold, the bridegroom is coming; go
out to meet him!' Then all those virgins arose and
trimmed their lamps. And the foolish said to the wise,
'Give us some of your oil, for our lamps are going out.'
But the wise answered, saying, 'No, lest there should not
be enough for us and you; but go rather to those who
sell, and buy for yourselves.' And while they went to buy,
the bridegroom came, and those who were ready went in
with him to the wedding; and the door was shut. After-
ward the other virgins came also, saying, 'Lord, Lord,
open to us!' But he answered and said, 'Assuredly, I say
to you, I do not know you.' Watch therefore, for you
know neither the day nor the hour in which the Son of
Man is coming." (Matt. 25:1-13)

This parable deals with the inward attitude of the believer.
Again, the cause of stumbling was the "tarrying of the bridegroom."

Matthew relates several parables in his gospel. There are parables concerning the founding of the kingdom. There are others
that speak of its character. A third group, to which this one belongs, tells of its consummation. In particular, this parable
brings forward some lessons from an earlier one, that of the
marriage feast (Matt. 22:1-14). In that previous parable, a man

without a wedding garment is cast out. The present parable builds on this principle. Both parables look to the future and the final consummation. Both teach that not all who are called will partake of the glories of that Day. Both teach that each individual is personally responsible, and each must individually prepare.

The parable of the ten virgins now extends these concepts further, emphasizing in this instance, lack of oil instead of failure to wear a wedding garment. The result is the same in both stories. The illustration of oil is used to emphasize the need for individual, personal, and spiritual preparation. Only such a mindset will endure "delay" and be unaffected by it. Each must be personally prepared for a lengthy delay by going to Christ directly. It illustrates issues already raised in Christ's earlier discourse (Matt. 24:36-51) where He spoke of the consequences of delay and the unexpectedness of His coming. Be constantly and personally prepared!

One of the central truths taught in this parable is the necessity of care and forethought to endure delay. In the end, one must have grace in order to welcome the advent of Christ. As in all the parables, the hour of arrival is uncertain and not as speedy as expected. The five virgins were foolish because they did not prepare for any endurance.

One must have "oil" for the duration. Beginnings are not enough; endings are vitally important as well. Oil may represent truth, which is obtained at a price: faith, prayer, and earnestness. How many times do believers miss opportunities to buy oil when it is easy? These people tend to live on present excitement rather than to prepare for the long haul.

Oil is obviously a symbol of the Holy Spirit. Growth and development in the Spirit of God must take place now, and each one must have his own lamp. The neglectful sin of the five virgins is the assumption that there would be plenty of oil in the common store in the house. In other words, these people simply live from the overflow of others and do not personally have devotional lives. They do not study scriptures on their own initiative; they do not work at personal relationships with the Lord; they have no prayer lives; and they live from the supply of others in the church.

These foolish people have no conception of personal obligation or of the very short interval between the arrival of the bridegroom and the closing of the door. There is no time to make up for present neglect. Lost ground will not be recovered at that point. The long delay causes some to become slack, and lose sight of the end for which they are to prepare themselves. The foolish virgins thought it was unnecessary to supply their own oil. Why bother with the cost when it is abundant in others?

In other words, these people make a profession and are expecting Christ's return, but they have made no personal preparation concerning grace or personal holiness. Their false assumption is that the need would be supplied simply by sitting in as a member of the church. Nevertheless, the oil must be their own, not someone else's.

Although the call was not unexpected, the five were unprepared. They were professors, but they did not practice the will of God. In the end, Jesus did not know them. These are the hypocrites, or the evil people. They had been awakened, but they had not prepared for the end!

Thought Questions

1. What is meant by the statement "The end is not yet"?

2. What is your understanding of the terms justification, sanctification, and glorification?

3. "The loss of the future dimension of salvation creates disturbing trends in the Body of Christ." How did these "disturbing trends" eventually affect the Body of Christ?

4. What should the "evil" servant (Matt. 24: 45-51) have done to avoid his undesirable end?

5. "Take heed to yourself and to the doctrine. Continue in them, for in doing this you will save both yourself and those who hear you." (1 Tim. 4:16). Paul admonishes Timothy regarding the present and the future. Discuss Paul's statement.

6. Suggest some similarities in the concepts Jesus taught in the parables of the Absent Goodman and the Ten Virgins.

7. Suggest a major difference in the concepts Jesus taught in the parables of the Absent Goodman and the Ten Virgins.

Chapter Fourteen

True servants find satisfaction in entering into the heart of the Master. The faithful are given opportunities for higher service and find in that service their satisfying rewards. The rewards are what the saints become, not what they get: it is the development of powers that fit Christians for higher service.

Hope Deferred - The End is Not Yet (Pt. II)

The Talents

"For the kingdom of heaven is like a man traveling to a far country, who called his own servants and delivered his goods to them. And to one he gave five talents, to another two, and to another one, to each according to his own ability; and immediately he went on a journey. Then he who had received the five talents went and traded with them, and made another five talents. And likewise he who had received two gained two more also. But he who had received one went and dug in the ground, and hid his lord's money. After a long time the lord of those servants came and settled accounts with them. So he who had received five talents came and brought five other talents, saying, 'Lord, you delivered to me five talents; look, I have gained five more talents besides them.' His lord said to him, 'Well done, good and faithful servant; you were faithful over a few things, I will make you ruler over many things. Enter into the joy of your lord.' He also who had received two talents came and said, 'Lord, you delivered to me two talents; look, I have gained two

more talents besides them.' His lord said to him, 'Well done, good and faithful servant; you have been faithful over a few things, I will make you ruler over many things. Enter into the joy of your lord.' Then he who had received the one talent came and said, 'Lord, I knew you to be a hard man, reaping where you have not sown, and gathering where you have not scattered seed. And I was afraid, and went and hid your talent in the ground. Look, there you have what is yours.' But his lord answered and said to him, 'You wicked and lazy servant, you knew that I reap where I have not sown, and gather where I have not scattered seed. So you ought to have deposited my money with the bankers, and at my coming I would have received back my own with interest. Therefore take the talent from him, and give it to him who has the ten talents. For to everyone who has, more will be given, and he will have abundance; but from him who does not have, even what he has will be taken away. And cast the unprofitable servant into the outer darkness. There will be weeping and gnashing of teeth.' " (Matt. 25:14-30)

This parable advances the previous lesson even further. The story of the ten virgins deals with the inner life, with personal preparation and application being the emphasis. However, faith without works is dead (James 2:26). Therefore, this parable addresses the need for external works, emphasizing accountability for endowment received.

As in the other parables, the cause of failure is the long absence of the master. The intended lesson is obvious. The Lord had ascended and will be gone for a much longer time than originally anticipated by His followers. Before leaving, He set His house in order and issued instructions to His servants (slaves). The Lord's affairs were entrusted to His disciples. They were to go to all nations with the gospel. Each was given trusts, which were to be managed for the Lord's interest and gain. These trusts were not given for safe custody, but for enlargement.

Many times, because of the long absence of the Master, the effect of His commands wears off. Sight of the Master's interests wanes. Nevertheless, there is work to be done. Slaves do not work for themselves, but for their master: no interest of God is carried forward without the labor of men. This parable indicated the Lord's desire for the church in the interim between the inauguration and the consummation of the kingdom of heaven.

The talents that the Lord gives are not trifles, but His gifts - anointings, character traits, and opportunities – are granted to each individual. They are to be administered for the Master's advantage. Important to note is the fact that the Lord has granted gifts to every person according to his abilities. This agrees wholeheartedly with the rest of the New Testament (1 Cor. 12:7; 2 Cor. 8:12; Heb. 2:4). God has distributed gifts to all, but not all have the same gifts. They are given according to what one can handle, according to the servant's capacity to use that trust. In this case, one received five talents, another was given two, and the third was entrusted with one.

The surprising detail in this story is that the one who had the least responsibility was the one who failed! Compared to the gifts of the others, he thought his one talent was insignificant, and that the master was rich enough already! He shunned the labor and responsibilities, forgetting from whom the talent came. The other two, who had received five and two talents, put in equal labor, devotion and faithfulness, and produced proportionately equal returns. At the time of reckoning, their rewards were equal. In the determination of the rewards their different abilities appeared to be insignificant; however, the effort expended proved to be of paramount importance.

After a long time, the master of the house returned: this is the main point of the story. Since the reckoning seemed far off, work in the present may have slackened. While the long delay provided time for development and gaining profit opportunities for the Master and His kingdom, it permitted some to be careless and negligent, actually increasing guilt on the day of reckoning. Conversely, to be about the Father's business will give boldness in that day (1 John 2:28).

The joy of the Master is communicated to the faithful. Those who have used their lives for the Master's gain are called good and faithful servants. They are good because they have exercised their trust for the benefit of others; they are faithful, because they were true to the Master's interests.

True servants find satisfaction in entering into the heart of the Master. The faithful are given opportunities for higher service and find in that service their satisfying rewards. The rewards are what the saints become, not what they get: it is the development of powers that fit Christians for higher service.

Work for the Master in the interim period is preparation for service in eternity. It is not only the believer's duty but also his joy and privilege. Satisfaction comes because of the heart sympathy with the aims and goals of the Master and the honor of participating in them. The reward is not sharing in a banquet meal to honor the believer, nor is it just a promotion. The present reward is training for service throughout eternity.

How is it that he who had received the one talent was unprepared for the day of reckoning? His task was the easiest. Therefore, his neglect was the more inexcusable. He entertained an incorrect view of the master, who would reckon the least service as something done to him. The servant brought charges against the lord, saying that the lord gained his riches by toil of others, and he expected gain without effort. This man obviously had himself in the centre of his thinking. Did he judge the character of his lord according to his own? He lacked joyous sympathy with the cause of his master and had a wrong view of the lord's work. God does not give gifts that fail. Failure comes because of the servant's unbelief!

In reality, he was afraid. This was an excuse built on the wrongful estimation of the master's character. He dared not take a chance of losing the trust that had been given. His excuse showed that he tried to cast the blame from himself to the master. He had hidden the talent. There was no recognition of duty to his master who had given the talent. His insolence became apparent when he tried to give back his unused talent. Hidden away, it was wasted. He is reckoned as a wicked servant because of his wrong description of the master; he is considered to be lazy because he put forth no effort to improve what had been entrusted to him.

Judgment will come forth out of his own mouth. If his description of the master were accurate, wouldn't his actions have been different? He will be judged according to his estimate of the master's character. If he feared loss by trading, did he not realize there are safe ways of gaining interest? Couldn't it have been deposited in the bank and gained interest in that way? Surely this is less work than digging a hole in the ground!

The believer who neglects spiritual gifts, considering them of little significance, exhibits the same character deficiencies that were evident in the one-talent servant. He quenches the Spirit and does not stir up the gifts. He has no sympathy with the cause of the Master for which the gifts are given. God gives gifts for them to be multiplied.

On the day of reckoning, even the little is taken away from the slothful. He will lose even if he has nothing of any consequence. God's work will not go undone. It will be given to another.

The parable reinforces the idea that grace used produces more grace. He who brought gain to the master now received even more. The believer's spiritual ability is developed by being properly directed. Present life is a stewardship. It is training for eternity. The future, as taught in the prophecy of the dividing of the sheep and the goats, is being made now. God has invested much in each believer. His Son died upon a cross. The Holy Spirit has been poured out. The Lord has determined each person's upbringing and environment. All servants, whatever the circumstances, must personally and directly use God's giftings to make gain for Christ during His long absence. Faithful use of these gifts opens fresh opportunities. Those who employ what is received will be given more; those who spurn will lose all.

Like the five foolish virgins, the lazy servant is put out where there is weeping and gnashing of teeth. For his neglect, laziness, and idleness, he is cast out and is filled with remorse.

The Sheep and the Goats

"When the Son of Man comes in His glory, and all the holy angels with Him, then He will sit on the throne of His glory. All the nations will be gathered before Him, and He will separate them one from another, as a shepherd divides his sheep from the goats. And He will set the sheep on His right hand, but the goats on the left. Then the King will say to those on His right hand, 'Come you blessed of My Father, inherit the kingdom prepared for you from the foundation of the world: for I was hungry and you gave Me food; I was thirsty and you gave Me drink; I was a stranger and you took Me in; I was

naked and you clothed Me; I was sick and you visited Me; I was in prison and you came to Me.' Then the righteous will answer Him saying, 'Lord, when did we see You hungry and feed You, or thirsty and give You drink? When did we see You a stranger and take You in, or naked and clothe You? Or when did we see You sick, or in prison, and come to You?' And the King will answer and say to them, 'Assuredly, I say to you, inasmuch as you did it to one of the least of these My brethren, you did it to Me.' Then He will also say to those on the left hand, 'Depart from Me, you cursed, into the everlasting fire prepared for the devil and his angels: for I was hungry and you gave Me no food; I was thirsty and you gave Me no drink; I was a stranger and you did not take Me in; naked and you did not clothe Me, sick and in prison and you did not visit Me.' Then they also will answer Him, saying, 'Lord, when did we see You hungry or thirsty or a stranger or naked or sick or in prison, and did not minister to You?' Then He will answer them saying, 'Assuredly, I say to you, inasmuch as you did not do it to one of the least of these, you did not do it to Me.' And these will go away into everlasting punishment, but the righteous into eternal life." (Matt. 25:31-46)

Jesus' discourse in Matthew 24 concerning the delay of the end and the three parables speaking of its evil consequences in the life of a faithless believer is brought to its sharp focus and conclusion in this prophetic description of the last day. The parables of the absent goodman, the ten virgins, and the talents now yield to this prophetic glimpse of the consummation of the kingdom. This is a statement of the future proceedings at the judgment.

Throughout his gospel, Matthew prepares his readers against the judgment to come. Presently in the kingdom, wheat and tares, good and bad fish, the just and the wicked, and sheep and goats exist together. During this time, the natural eye cannot distinguish one from the other. At the end, the true character of everyone will be seen. Separation will forever be made. The professor of the will of God will be distinguished from the doer. Not all who claim to be followers of Christ will be able to say that they indeed did follow Him. There will be those who cry out, "Lord," in that day, but will be turned away forever.

When Jesus spoke these parables, He was only a few days away from going to the cross, but He looked forward through time to the conclusion of the kingdom in the dispensation of time, to the introduction of eternity. His thoughts envision the end of that which he inaugurated by His death and resurrection.

In the parable of the ten virgins, the inner life and faith of the individual believers are examined. However, as Matthew's gospel constantly underlines, faith without works is dead. Therefore, the parable of the talents follows, emphasizing the outer life and works that shall be judged on the final day. Now the scene is widened to the great judgment of the whole world.

All of creation is summoned and gathered by the angels to this final judgment. None is exempt. All who ever lived are now present to give account. This final judgment is according to works, thus giving the previous parables more weight. Faith that does not produce works is not faith. Faith is active, not just mere mental assent. He who sits on the throne will not ask what anyone has believed, thought or felt. More importantly He will ask what one has done to advance the work of the Lord. What has been the individual's conduct in the world?

Though the final judgment is according to works, these works, as this prophecy teaches, spring out of faith and derive their whole spiritual value from the faith and love that prompted them. The faith that shapes a person's life is visible by the good works performed under the Lord's direction.

The scene of the closing out of time is brought before Matthew's readers. Christ is in His glory; his state of humiliation has passed away. This is the only time in scripture that Christ refers to Himself as King. As Jesus had earlier spoken (Matt. 24:30-31), the angels have gathered together the elect from the four winds, from one end of heaven to the other. All the nations have been summoned. Of angels and men, none is absent. Christ sits upon His glorious throne before all creation.

Only two classes of people will be seen on that day. The sheep will be assigned to the right, the place of honor and favor. The goats are assigned to the left, the place of rejection and dishonor.

At first, no explanation for the division is given. Only after complete separation has been achieved is sentence pronounced. The rewards are spoken first. The King invites those on the right to "Come." Those who had responded to the call "Come to Me" during the days of Christ's humiliation now hear Him call to them as He sits on His throne of glory. He who has the kingdom by right now invites the righteous to possess the kingdom in its glory with Him. They are blessed of the Father, because they had used the grace given to them and had cooperated with the Holy Spirit. They do not just "take" the kingdom; they "inherit" it, becoming joint-heirs with the One who sits on the throne. The kingdom was "prepared" from the foundation of the world. History has been moving to this very climax!

The righteous are astonished at this invitation and unaware of their worthiness for such glory. How did they qualify? The Lord upon the throne speaks of works of mercy, which are proofs of self-denial, pity, sympathy, and love. These works of mercy demonstrate that the doer of the works has the influence of God in him and has exercised the grace of love. The righteous do not know until this final day the preciousness of acts of kindness in the Lord's sight.

This scripture identifies the Lord with human frailty (Isa. 53:4; 63:9). The Lord is one with His creation. Having become flesh, Christ is one with mankind. Had Matthew's readers ceased to look on humanity as the Lord's brethren?

Now the Lord addresses those on the left hand with the word "Depart." To hear those words from the One who loves souls and died for them must be bitter indeed. They were cursed. Note that it does not say "Cursed of My Father" for it is not God's heart to do such. They are assigned, not to the kingdom prepared for the Lord, but to everlasting fire that was prepared for the devil and his angels. God had not prepared it for men!

Where had these gone wrong? They had not the love of God, though they might be professors of faith. Their omission and negligence proved their unprofitable lives. How dwells the love of God in such? In reality, they did not know God, Who is love.

Those on the left are sent to everlasting punishment, having never known the Lord. Their actions, or lack thereof, deny Him. Who can fathom the horribleness of such a sentence? Everlasting punishment! Weeping and gnashing of teeth!

The righteous enter their eternal reward: eternal life, joint-heirs with Christ in His eternal glorious kingdom!

Thought Questions

1. Each of the three servants received a different number of talents from their lord. The servants who invested their talents and gained profit equal to the investments were given the same commendation. Why do you think the two-talent servant did not receive a lesser reward than the five-talent servant?

2. Obviously, the one-talent servant did not attempt to make a profit for his lord. Why was he content to leave his talent buried in the ground?

3. Whom does the Lord refer to as "good and faithful servants?"

4. *"Therefore take the talent from him* (one-talent servant), *and give it to him who has the ten talents."* This quote (Matt. 25:28) bears an important message for Christians today. What admonition does it offer?

5. The righteous did not know until the final day the preciousness of acts of kindness in the Lord's sight. How do the righteous gain this information?

Hope Deferred- The End is Not Yet (Pt. II)

Chapter Fifteen

> *In the meantime, the church learns and practices righteous behavior. The believer is to give faithful service as a steward in the Lord's absence. Each must buy oil now for all night burning. The gifts given by Christ are to be traded in the marketplace to bring Him profit that He claims at His return. The church must be busy doing works of mercy, seeing all mankind as the brethren of the Lord.*

Matthew's Remedy

How is hope to be restored to the church? What prescription does Matthew give to remedy the disillusionment that delayed hope has created?

To answer this, Matthew consistently brings forth two features of Christ. In one short statement, Matthew portrays the **servant** and the **kingly** aspects of the Messiah. The One who lowered himself in His humiliation is the same as the majestic One:

> *"And suddenly a voice came from heaven, saying, 'This is My beloved Son, in whom I am well pleased.' "* (Matt. 3:17 – Son and Servant)

When giving this pronouncement, God the Father quotes from two Old Testament prophecies (Ps. 2:7 & Isa. 42:1). By looking at these prophecies, it is observed that the first quote reveals the kingly aspect of His Son, while the second quote describes His service.

Christ is the Messiah. His ancestry and lineage are provided in Matt. 1:1-17. The prophets foretold His entire life and ministry. Jesus' birth was miraculous. Magi visited and worshiped Him (Matt. 2:1-11). Matthew only recorded events worthy of a king: in relating the birth of Jesus, he did not record anything about the manger or shepherds.

He triumphantly entered Jerusalem (Matt. 21:1-11). On more than one occasion, the Father testified from heaven that Christ is His son (Matt. 3:17; 17:5). He is the chosen one, the elect (Matt. 12:18). He is Immanuel (Matt. 1:23), Son of David (Matt. 1:1; 9:27; 12:23; 15:22; 22:41-46), Son of Abraham (Matt. 1:1), Son of Man (Matt. 8:20; 26:64), Son of God (Matt. 16:16). Christ is the anointed one who heals the sick and casts out demons, bringing near the kingdom of heaven (Matt. 4:23 –25; 12:28).

Nonetheless, besides these regal claims, Matthew equally emphasizes the lowliness and humiliation of Christ. He is obedient to His Father and content to submit to whatever is fitting to fulfill all righteousness (Matt. 3:15), even carrying infirmities and sickness (Matt. 8:17). He is the lowly King mounted upon a donkey (Matt. 21:7-11). Children surround Him (Matt. 18:2; 19:13-15). He refers to Himself as meek and lowly in heart (Matt. 11:29). The leaders of His day attack Him. His words are not understood and obeyed. He is accused of being Beelzebub (Matt. 12:24). Peter rebuked Him (Matt. 16:22); Judas betrayed Him (Matt. 26:25). He was mocked, scourged, and crucified (Matt. 27:26-31). He was without honor (Matt. 13:53-58).

Matthew saw Jesus as the Son of David and at the same time David's Lord. He is both the humble One and the mighty One (Matt. 22:41-46). While he cast out demons by the Spirit of God, he was accused of being the prince of demons (Matt. 12:22-30). This contrast of the different sides of Christ is true to fact.

What did Matthew intend to teach by portraying Christ in this manner? Christ was to be seen "in process," passing through different phases. Though He willingly accepted His humiliation, the day will come when He will be seen in a different light:

> *"For the Son of Man will come in the glory of His Father with His angels, and then He will reward each according to his works."* (Matt. 16:27)

His humiliation will be laid aside forever. The glory revealed at the transfiguration was a foretaste of that (Matt. 17:1-8):

> *"and He was transformed before them. His face shone like the sun, and His clothes became as white as the light. And behold, Moses and Elijah appeared to them, talking with Him."* (Matt. 17:2-3)

Christ testified, as a prisoner before the high priest Caiaphas, that He will be beheld in a very different light as the Son of Man sitting on the right hand of power, coming in the clouds of heaven:

> *"Jesus said to him, 'It is as you said. Nevertheless, I say to you, hereafter you will see the Son of Man sitting at the right hand of the Power, and coming on the clouds of heaven."* (Matt. 26:64)

After His resurrection, the church recognizes Christ as both the lowly and the exalted One who has all authority in heaven and earth. The same One is yet to be seen as the coming One at the end of time, appearing with His angels in the glory of His Father. He will acknowledge His own before the Father. He is returning at an hour that no one knows and will send His angels with a trumpet blast to gather all to the judgment. At that time, He will take account with His servants.

There will be a final unveiling of the Messiah's glory! The coming in glory of the exalted Christ is simply the climax of the revelation of Jesus. It is necessary that Christ should come again to complete His work: to consummate the kingdom that has been inaugurated (Matt. 4:17), to finish the believer's salvation, and to perfect the church's knowledge of Him (Matt. 25:31). All is still incomplete. This is Matthew's prescription for disillusionment. Though the believer is still in his humiliation, he will be glorified with Christ on that Day! As Christ was, so the believer is "in process." Church, look forward!

The future belongs to Christ. That destiny is God's to unfold. The reins of history are held in His hands, but no one knows the manner or the time of the end. According to Matthew, ignorance prompts alertness. From Matthew's perspective, the believer does not live in an orderly, predictable world in which the future is blueprinted, prepackaged, and predetermined by unalterable laws. No one knows! Matthew's view is that the believer lives among miracles in an unpredictable world with God present, and the future is wide open all the time. No one knows how it will all happen (Matt. 24:36-44; 25:13)!

What the church does know, however, is that her destiny is altogether bound up in the advent of Christ. The church now knows the risen Christ in the midst of the church's humiliation. At Christ's advent, the church participates in His glory and kingdom.

Matthew's doctrine states that during the present the future is made; therefore, this sure victory should not lull the church into idle waiting. In the meantime, the church learns and practices righteous behavior. The believer is to give faithful service as a steward in the Lord's absence. Each must buy oil now for all night burning. The gifts given by Christ are to be traded in the marketplace to bring Him profit that He claims at His return.

The church must be busy doing works of mercy, seeing all mankind as the brethren of the Lord. All this is done in the confidence that the future is "made." Each believer is to prepare against it and to be fashioned by the Lord in preparation for it. God has unforeseeable good in store. The sure hope is that he who endures to the end will be saved and that the arriving One will say, "Come, you blessed of My Father, inherit the kingdom prepared for you from the foundation of the world."

Thought Questions

1. What was Matthew's purpose in portraying the kingly and servant aspects of the Messiah?

2. Matthew saw Jesus as the Son of David and at the same time David's Lord. Comment on this statement.

3. What should the church, having the confidence that the future is "made," be doing while Jesus' return is delayed?

4. Describe how the believer appears in the world today, and how he shall appear on the final day.

Section VI.

The Beatitudes

Section VI

Chapter Sixteen

> *The first need of grace in our lives is to see the holiness of God. Then we must have an understanding of our needs. Revelation of the holiness of God and of man's desperate need of God's grace become the foundation for other graces to be worked in our lives. This should be the first effect of having the Law written on the tables of our hearts.*

The Beatitudes

*"And seeing the multitudes, He went up on a mountain, and when He was seated His disciples came to Him. Then He opened His mouth and taught them, saying: 'Blessed are the **poor in spirit**, For theirs is the kingdom of heaven. Blessed are those who **mourn**, For they shall be comforted. Blessed are **the meek**, For they shall inherit the earth. Blessed are those who **hunger and thirst for righteousness**, For they shall be filled. Blessed are the **merciful**, For they shall obtain **mercy**. Blessed are the **pure in heart**, For they shall see God. Blessed are the **peacemakers**, For they shall be called the sons of God. Blessed are those who are **persecuted for righteousness' sake**, For theirs is the kingdom of heaven."* (Matt. 5:1-10)

Often, the Beatitudes are called the New Testament counterpart of the Old Testament Ten Commandments. Just as Exodus (the giving of the Law) follows Genesis (the beginnings), so in Matthew, the commentary of the Law follows the beginnings of the gospel. Obviously, the Beatitudes are not new commandments. They do not present to us the observance of the Law written on tables of stone; however, they do illustrate the realization and effects of the Law written by the Spirit on the tables of our hearts.

Christ has no conflict with the Law; indeed, He came to fulfill it. However, Jesus detests the Pharisaic version of it. He provides the Law's rightful interpretation, rescuing it from the Pharisees' perversion (Matt. 5:17-20). In His teaching, Jesus describes proper righteousness for us. Just as Moses begins to interpret the Ten Commandments of Exodus 20 by examples in Exodus 21 and 22, Jesus first shows the effects of the Law revealed in the heart (Matt. 5: 1-20) and then follows this with its application in life's situations (Matt. 5: 21-48). Exodus 19:3-6 acts as a prologue to the Ten Commandments, and Matthew 5:13-16 acts as an epilogue to the Beatitudes.

Throughout the entire Sermon on the Mount, Jesus contrasts His interpretation of Moses with that of the current teaching of the scribes and Pharisees. The subject matter is the kingdom of heaven. To the Jews, the arrival of the Messiah and the kingdom means the conquering of political enemies. It is thoroughly external and often desired by fiery, impure enthusiasm eager for gross delights and vulgar conquests. The kingdom that Jesus brings is a spiritual reality now, consisting of righteousness and grace progressively learned under the authority of God. It carries a reward in the future at the appearing of Christ.

Clearly, the nature of the kingdom and its righteousness is a great point of dispute between Jesus and the scribes and Pharisees. Sin and temptation, personal feelings, marriage, discipleship, and many other topics are viewed quite differently.

Humility is handled in another manner. Jesus teaches humility as a despairing of self. The scribes and Pharisees think of it as the consciousness of failure or inadequate perfectness. (It was really pride.)

Perfection also receives different treatment. The rabbis teach that perfection is arrived at by the external means of working to become a child of God. Jesus starts at the goal of the rabbis (perfection), but He bestows a new life as a child of God at the beginning of the Christian life. Jesus defines perfection as a new life springing from God and in God.

It is with this understanding that we approach the Beatitudes. As Gideon tested his men regarding the manner in which they drank water, so the Beatitudes test us to determine whether carnal good is uppermost in our hearts.

Jesus uses the word "blessed" throughout. It is the Greek word "makarios" meaning a "god-like joy" that has its secret within itself. It is serene and untouchable, completely independent of outside forces. It is not "happiness" which is contingent on "happenings." In another place (John 16:22), Jesus says that man is incapable of taking away this joy from its possessor. Indeed, no outer force can touch this joy that keeps us through the storms and discomforts of life.

In the Greek, the word "are" following the word "blessed" is not there (Blessed are). Notice the word is in italics. This means that the word was supplied by the translators of the King James Version for smoother reading in English. Realizing that the word "are" is not in the original sayings of Jesus throughout the Beatitudes, one can see that the Beatitudes are not statements as much as exclamations! To the modern reader, it is as if Jesus is exclaiming, "Oh, the blessedness of ..." He congratulates what is!

Christ does not refer to rewards that can be attained but rather to an inherent state enjoyed now, bestowed by the grace of God.

In the Beatitudes, especially the first two, Jesus opens to us the meaning of repentance. It is the sum of His message (Matt. 4:17). Repentance is the beginning of the Christian life, and the Spirit of God must work this thoroughly in our hearts. We must be truly convicted of sin (which is one of the functions of the Law) as well as the unworthiness of our flesh. Consider man's sinful nature, what he is in the flesh. He became filled with himself when he ate of the tree of the knowledge of good and evil (Gen. 2 & 3). The Beatitudes describe the emptying of self from man.

The Beatitudes illustrate life in the kingdom of heaven. The first (Matt. 5:3) and the last (Matt. 5:10) Beatitudes state the kingdom of heaven belongs to those who are described therein. The Beatitudes show how entry is made into the kingdom of heaven and how life is lived in the kingdom. Preaching the gospel of the kingdom produces these effects in the hearer. The eight Beatitudes are divided into two groups of four, each ending with the theme of righteousness (Matt. 5:6,10).

The first group of four shows how entry is made into the kingdom of heaven, while the second group of four shows subsequent fruit demonstrated after entry has been made. A ninth Beatitude is then spoken as a direct application to the hearers (Matt. 5:11). Jesus changed his sayings to "Blessed are you" from "Blessed are they."

Thought Questions

1. How did the kingdom of heaven Jesus inaugurated differ from the Jewish concept of the kingdom?

2. The word "blessed" begins each of the Beatitudes. As it is used in the Beatitudes, what is the meaning of the word "blessed?"

3. How do the Beatitudes describe life in the kingdom of heaven?

4. Into what two divisions can the Beatitudes be divided?

The Beatitudes

Chapter Seventeen

> *Poverty of spirit is not just God's opinion: the teaching of the Law has been our undoing, and now it is our opinion, too.*

"Blessed are the poor in spirit, For theirs is the kingdom of heaven." (Matt. 5:3)

This Beatitude reflects the opposite of the Jewish mindset that considered being poor in spirit in a negative manner. If a man lowered himself, he would become the food of worms.

The first need of grace in our lives is to see the holiness of God. Then we must have an understanding of our needs. Revelation of the holiness of God and of man's desperate need of God's grace become the foundation for other graces to be worked in our lives. This should be the first effect of having the Law written on the tables of our hearts. The first few Beatitudes remind the believer of the wonderful promise of the Spirit's work as shown in the famous prophecy of Isaiah 61:1-3. In this prophetic promise, those who are poor and mourn receive the good tidings of the gospel and may expect to receive the floodtide of the Holy Spirit, the Comforter!

To be poor in spirit is to be empty of self, to wait for God. It is a sense of unworthiness in contrast to self-sufficiency and self-assertiveness (c.f. Rev. 3:17). This quality is the exact opposite the Jewish frame of mind that Jesus found during His days upon the earth (c.f. Rom. 2:17-24).

One of the great purposes of the Law is to reveal our sinfulness. This was evidenced in the story of the rich young ruler (Matt. 19:16-22). Correctly understood, the Law reveals the corruptness of the heart. Who can read Jesus' teaching on the Law in Matthew 5:21-48 and not be convicted? Later, Paul the Apostle also speaks of the purpose of the Law, especially in his epistle to the Romans:

> *"... for **by the law** is the knowledge of sin."* (Rom. 3:20)

> *"because the law brings about wrath; **for where there is no law there is no transgression.**"* (Rom. 4:15)

> *"For until the law sin was in the world, but **sin is not imputed when there is no law.**"* (Rom. 5:13)

> *"Moreover the **law entered that the offense might abound.**"* (Rom. 5:20)

> *"I would **not have known sin except through the law,**"* (Rom. 7:7)

When the Holy Spirit thoroughly applies the righteousness of the Law to our hearts, we are convinced of both our utter helplessness and lack of resources. We see our sins before a holy God. More than that, we also see ourselves as wrong. What we "are," not just what we "do", is sick. We become overwhelmed with a consciousness of our spiritual deficiency.

The spirit is the highest and most noble part of man. This poverty of "spirit" describes life as lived before and unto God. It is the spirit of man that feels after God; it is in the spirit that the poverty is acutely felt. Within ourselves, we are void of the God-kind of life. Poverty of spirit is not just God's opinion: the teaching of the Law has been our undoing, and now it is our opinion, too. Poverty of spirit penetrates our consciousness about ourselves, and we welcome the Spirit's help in our lives.

Greek, the original language of the New Testament, provides two words for the English word "poor." The word used in Matthew 5:3 is "ptochos." The other word that is not used here, "penes," describes a man who has to work for a living. He is neither penniless nor superfluous in lifestyle. However, the word "ptochos" used in the Beatitudes means abject and absolute poverty. Its root word (ptossein) means to crouch or to cower. The poor man has nothing at all; his is a poverty that beats a man to his knees. This kind of poverty needs to be realized in our spirits before a holy God. The work of the Holy Spirit is to apply the righteous demands of a righteous God to hearts that are hardened. The truth of God is like a hammer that breaks the rock in pieces (Jer. 23:29). This is the first step that God takes to remove our stony hearts and to give us hearts of flesh (Ezek. 36:26-27).

There are two Hebrew words for poor (ani and ebion). The Jews had a special way of using these words. In time, the word "poor" went through changes in meaning. The development is as follows:

A) A man was poor.
B) Because he was poor, he had no influence, power, help, or prestige.
C) Because he failed to influence, he became downtrodden and oppressed by men.
D) Because he had no earthly resources, he put his whole trust in God.

Jesus uses this final and full meaning (D) concerning poverty of spirit, and it is the sense of many cries of the Old Testament saints. Jesus draws from the background of these cries to teach about the entry into the kingdom of heaven:

*"**This poor man cried out, and the Lord heard him,** And saved him out of all his troubles."* (Ps. 34:6)

*"For the needy shall not always be forgotten; **The expectation of the poor shall not perish forever."*** (Ps. 9:18)

*"All my bones shall say, 'Lord, who is like You, Delivering the poor from him who is too strong for him, Yes**, the poor and the needy from him who plunders him?'** "* (Ps. 35:10)

*"But I am poor and needy; Yet the Lord thinks upon me. **You are my help and my deliverer**; Do not delay, O my God."* (Ps. 40:17)

*"For the **Lord hears the poor**, And does not despise his prisoners."* (Ps. 69:33)

*"**He will bring justice to the poor of the people**; He will save the children of the needy, And will break in pieces the oppressor."* (Ps. 72:4)

*"**He will spare the poor and needy**, And will save the souls of the needy."* (Ps. 72:13)

*"Yet **He sets the poor on high**, far from affliction, And makes their families like a flock."* (Ps. 107:41)

*"I will abundantly bless her provision; **I will satisfy her poor with bread.**"* (Ps. 132:15)

*" 'For all those things My hand has made, And all those things exist,' Says the Lord. But on this one will I look: **On him who is poor and of a contrite spirit**, And who trembles at My word."* (Is. 66:2)

Jesus applies this understanding of the word "poor" to man's standing before God. Already, Isaiah had used the term to describe man's spiritual condition before God. Having this illumination from the Holy Spirit, as evidenced by the righteousness of the Law, the man who is poor in spirit has his conscience awakened to his utter helplessness and lack of resources. Therefore he trusts not himself, but puts his whole trust in God alone. He realizes that he can do nothing and has need of all things. The work of the Holy Spirit bringing forth the righteousness of God as exemplified in His righteous Law has produced a sense of emptiness within.

This is the beginning of repentance. Once seeing ourselves in the light of God, we realize that we cannot bring forward our fleshly wisdom, ideas, and strengths into the things of God. How we need to learn to distrust ourselves so that our trust will be in God alone! To such belongs the kingdom of heaven, for this is the way of entry!

This, too, is a comforting word for the believer, for with this comes the blessed realization that the whole Christian life is a gift. Faith, love, repentance, power, and all else that pertain to a walk with God are freely given in Christ. Without Him, we can produce nothing of eternal value, but in Christ we receive all things. What a glorious truth!

Thought Questions

1. Describe the *"poor in spirit"* as it is used in Matthew 5:3.

2. The blessed realization that the whole Christian life is a gift from God is comforting for the believer. Comment on this concept.

3. What are the meanings of the Hebrew and Greek words for "poor?"

4. Why is being poor in spirit the beginning of repentance?

Chapter Eighteen

> *This godly sorrow causes us to forsake all that the righteous Law has convicted us of previously. The hard ground is broken up so that we can now receive the seed of the Word and the rain of the Holy Spirit.*

"Blessed are they who mourn, For they shall be comforted." (Matt. 5:4)

This Beatitude also must have offended the Jewish mindset of the day, for to them misery in this world anticipates punishment later.

The second Beatitude, as the first, reminds us of Isaiah 61:1-3, where the declaration is made that mourners will be comforted.

There are various types of mourning, both good and bad: mourning over one's loss or wailing that self-pity demands. The Greek word used here describes someone mourning for the dead. Compare Jacob's remarks in Genesis 37:34-35. It is a grief that takes such a hold on man that it cannot be hidden. It is a sorrow that brings uncontrollable tears to the eyes.

Just as the first Beatitude is felt in the spirit, so is this mourning felt there. We have been awakened to feel our need and our lost condition! The Holy Spirit has so worked in us that we are desperately and intensely sorry for our sin. Grief over our unworthiness, our lack of gratitude, and our coldness of heart cause us to call out to God to deliver us from ourselves! Not only do we grieve over what sin has done to us, but also we become heartbroken over what our sin has done to God. The prodigal son first acknowledged that he had sinned against heaven (Luke 15:21) and the penitent King David recognized that his adulterous behavior was against God (Ps 51:4). The realization that our sin put Christ upon the cross produces intense sorrow.

This mourning feels not only the poverty in our own spirits but also the sin around us, making us intercessors. Scripture has many examples of mourning being poured out in prayer for others. Jesus wept over Jerusalem (Matt. 23:37-39). Horror gripped the Psalmist (Ps. 119:53). The prophets wept over the nation (Jer. 9:18; 13:17; 14:17; Lam. 2:11; Dan. 9:20; Ezek. 9:4; and Neh. 1:6-7).

Mourning seeks deliverance from the burden of sin. By breaking up the hardness of man's heart, it prepares and enables him to receive from God and to be cleared of anything that is offensive to God. It is the full fruit of repentance and is exemplified in 2 Cor. 7:10-11:

> *"For godly sorrow produces repentance leading to salvation, not to be regretted; but the sorrow of the world produces death. For observe this very thing, that you sorrowed in a godly manner:* **What diligence it produced in you, what clearing of yourselves, what indignation, what fear, what vehement desire, what zeal, what vindication!** *In all things you proved yourselves to be clear in this matter."*

This godly sorrow causes us to forsake all that the righteous Law has convicted us of previously. The hard ground is broken up so that we can now receive the seed of the Word and the rain of the Holy Spirit. The balm of Gilead now may be applied.

Those who mourn shall be comforted. The comfort is full forgiveness, freely given. David understood this when he said:

*"The sacrifices of God are a broken spirit, A broken and a contrite heart – **These, O God, You will not despise."** (Ps. 51:17)*

The word "they" is emphatic (Matt. 5:4). The blessing of being comforted belongs to no one else. Weeping turns into joy. Note these promises:

*"For His anger is but for a moment, His favor is for life; **Weeping may endure for a night, But joy comes in the morning."** (Ps. 30:5)*

*"To console those who mourn in Zion, **To give them beauty for ashes, the oil of joy for mourning, The garment of praise for the spirit of heaviness;** That they may be called trees of righteousness, The planting of the Lord, that He may be glorified."* (Is. 61:3)

*"Most assuredly, I say to you that you will weep and lament, but the world will rejoice; and you will be sorrowful, **but your sorrow will be turned into joy."*** (John 16:20)

It is of significant importance that the Holy Spirit is known as the Helper or Comforter (John 16:7). This ties in beautifully with Isaiah. For those who mourn, the comfort of the Holy Spirit will be given. This gives us an understanding of how one may experience the depths of the ministry of the Holy Spirit. Those who have been emptied through repentance, being poor in spirit and mourning, may expect a full measure of the power of the Holy Spirit in their lives and experience. Perhaps the lack of embracing these first two Beatitudes is the cause of anaemic Spirit-filled lives.

Poverty of spirit followed by mourning is the repentance worked in our hearts by the Holy Spirit bearing witness to the truth of God's righteousness as seen in the Law, especially in the Ten Commandments. It forms the basis of our initial conversion. Conversion is not just mental acceptance of fact, but it is being born again, having a change of life resulting from a change of heart.

The Greek word used for "mourn" in Matthew 5:4 is written in the continuous tense. Until Christ returns, at which time we will be glorified with Him, we must choose to live according to God's ways - not our own. We must not walk according to the flesh while still living in this present evil world. We must abide in this place of mourning over anything that proceeds from the flesh. Our conscience needs to be kept tender, and when we bring any carnal wisdom and strength into the things of God, we must be brought back to this place. As we have entered, so must we abide.

In scripture, there are some beautiful illustrations of this mourning that received comfort. How touching is the story of the woman who washed the feet of Jesus with her hair and received forgiveness (Luke 7:36-50)! Peter knew the anguish of soul after he betrayed Jesus (Matt. 26:75). It was the penitent publican, not the proud Pharisee, who left his prayer time justified (Luke 18:9-14). Listen to the Psalmist as he mourns over the sinful condition before God:

> *"For innumerable evils have surrounded me; My iniquities have overtaken me, so that I am not able to look up; They are more than the hairs of my head; Therefore my heart fails me.* **Be pleased, O Lord, to**

deliver me; O Lord, make haste to help me!" (Ps. 40:12-13)

"Have mercy on me, O Lord, for I am in trouble; My eye wastes away with grief, Yes, my soul and my body! For my life is spent with grief, And my years with sighing; ***My strength fails because of my iniquity, and my bones waste away."*** (Ps. 31:9-10)

"For I am ready to fall, And my sorrow is continually before me. ***For I will declare my iniquity; I will be in anguish over my sin."*** (Ps. 38:17-18)

Psalm 38 should be read in its entirety. Compare the word of the Lord as spoken through Hosea:

"I will return again to My place, Till they acknowledge their offense. Then will they seek My face; ***In their affliction they will earnestly seek Me."*** (Hos. 5:15)

Also in the Psalms one will find the comfort of which Jesus spoke. Following the mourning comes the forgiveness of sin. Psalm 34:18-22 is an example:

"The Lord is near to those who have a broken heart, And saves such as have a contrite spirit. ***Many are the afflictions of the righteous, but the Lord delivers him out of them all.*** *He guards all his bones; Not one of them is broken. Evil shall slay the wicked, And those who hate the righteous shall be condemned. The Lord redeems the soul of His servants, And none of those who trust in Him shall be condemned."*

All of Psalm 32 is an encouragement to read, showing that God forgives sin which one confesses. Part of the Psalm reads:

"When I kept silent, my bones grew old Through my groaning all the day long. For day and night Your hand was heavy upon me; My vitality was turned into the drought of summer. I acknowledged my sin to You, And my iniquity I have not hidden. I said, **'I will confess My transgressions to the Lord,' And You forgave the iniquity of my sin.***"* (Ps. 32:3-5)

There truly is comfort for those who mourn!

Thought Questions

1. Does Jacob's grief shown in Genesis 37:34-35 illustrate the kind of mourning described in this chapter? If so, express what you think Jesus meant when He said, *"Blessed are those who mourn."* (Matt. 5:4)

2. How does mourning lead to intercession?

3. Describe godly sorrow.

4. What is the biblical relationship between mourning and comfort?

Blessed Are Those Who Mourn

Chapter Nineteen

> *Meekness recognizes that God is break-*
> *ing our independence so that the tal-*
> *ents, capabilities, and powers with*
> *which we were created will not be*
> *wasted, but will come to full fruition. Sin*
> *and self have robbed us of our powers.*
> *This knowledge instills in us patience*
> *and contentment that foster a mild dis-*
> *position to those who are good to us and*
> *gentleness to the evil.*

"Blessed are the meek,
For they shall inherit the earth."
(Matt. 5:5)

Like the first two Beatitudes, the third also recalls Isaiah 61:1-3. The Biblical use of the word "meek" is not to be misconstrued because of its secular use. To the world, "meekness" tends to be understood in the sense of spinelessness, weakness, or subservience. It conjures up a picture of a person allowing himself to be trampled by others. This is unfortunate as the Biblical definition shows meekness to be the fruit of power. In the Greek language in which the original New Testament was written, the word translated "meekness" is one of great ethical connotation.

The placement of meekness relative to the other Beatitudes is important. Jesus is showing us the orderly development of grace (righteousness of the Law internalized) on the tables of our hearts. We have first a poverty of spirit, filling us with a sense of our nothingness and insufficiency before a holy and righteous

God. Secondly comes mourning, an intense sorrow over sin. Meekness then follows. Having clearly seen our sinful state and having repented of it, we become aware that we have nothing before God and are in need of all things. We have no wisdom except that which He grants.

The following may help us understand some of the many faces of meekness. Meekness is:

- the brokenness of our wills that makes the heart receptive to new instruction.
- the attitude that permits the receiving of the engrafted word that is able to save our souls (James 1:21).
- the attitude that allows the taming of the lion within us.
- the attitude of teachability such as a disciple should have toward his teacher.
- the disposition of a son learning from his father.
- the servant doing the bidding of his master.
- the acceptance of the necessity to learn.

Meekness is an inwrought grace that describes the condition of the heart, whereas gentleness is more descriptive of actions. The following excerpt from Psalm 25 exemplifies David's meekness of heart:

*"Do not remember the sins of my youth, nor my transgressions; According to Your mercy remember me, For Your goodness' sake, O Lord. Good and upright is the Lord; Therefore He teaches sinners in the way. **The humble He guides in justice, And the humble He teaches His way. All the paths of the Lord are mercy and truth, To such as keep His covenant and His testimonies.** For Your name's sake, O Lord, Pardon my iniquity, for it is great."* (Ps. 25:7-11)

Meekness is not weakness. Moses was the meekest or humblest man on the face of the earth (Num. 12:3) and yet, when the children of Israel made a golden calf (Ex. 32:19-20), he showed blazing anger when God's honor was not respected! Jesus called attention to His own meekness (Matt. 11:29; c.f. 2 Cor. 10:1), but He could also be very angry when confronted with religious hypocrisy (Matt. 23).

Meekness is power under control; meekness does not retaliate when it has the power to do so. It knows when to get angry and when to restrain anger. A meek man has mastery of all his passions and holds them in subjection to serve nobler purposes. For instance, we need to learn not to react when provoked. Meekness takes everything patiently and does not allow anger to arise when we are slighted or attacked. It does not desire to get even. Jesus gives examples of the fruit of meekness in the Sermon on the Mount in Matt. 5:21-26, 38-42.

However, there are things at which we should get angry. Hypocrisy should stir us as it did Jesus. We do need to get angry at sin and bondage. Properly engaged, anger can assist in breaking the chains of bondage, be regulated by faith, and be a bulwark to the soul.

Meekness accepts the dealings of God as good, without dispute or resistance. Mourning over poverty of spirit won't permit one to oppose the new instruction of God. It simply will not struggle, fight, or contend with God. Even if the discipline of God comes through the insults and injuries of evil men, meekness can accept them out of a sense that God has permitted it for the chastening and purifying of His people. Flesh sees the evil men and the unpleasant circumstances, but meekness sees God. We may discern evil and suffer it; we can be aware of everything, but meekness holds the reins. Because we see God, we can be gentle, especially toward the evil and unthankful. A prime example is the story of Joseph who was sold into slavery by his brothers. Later, when he had power to order their execution, he did not, for he saw the hand of God in it all (Gen. 45:5; 50:20). That is meekness, the fruit of power over one's self.

In the first three Beatitudes, Jesus describes characteristics of the heart that effectively remove hindrances to true spirituality. Pride is overcome when we are poor in spirit; thoughtlessness and levity are replaced with mourning; anger, impatience, and discontent are overruled by meekness.

Notice that hungering and thirsting after righteousness come after meekness. Before we can be filled with the righteousness of God, our self-will must be destroyed and our teachability immensely enhanced so that we can depend on God who said that His grace is sufficient for us. Meekness, then, is the acceptance that we are to learn at God's hands. It learns to see the hand of God in His allowances and manifests itself in a calm acquiescence to His will, even though it may not be pleasant. It says, "It is the Lord, let Him do what seems good to Him." This attitude creates a quiet and patient bearing. Before resisting the devil, one must first submit to God (James 4:7).

Perhaps this will be understood better if it is realized that the Greeks used the word for meekness (praus) to describe a wild horse that has been domesticated. For instance, a wild horse has tremendous capabilities and powers, but it is nonproductive. However, once it comes under the control of another, it can be amazingly useful. The horse must be "broken." Meekness recognizes that God is breaking our independence so that the talents, capabilities, and powers with which we were created will not be wasted, but will come to full fruition. Sin and self have robbed us of our powers. This knowledge instills in us patience and contentment that foster a mild disposition to those who are good to us and gentleness to the evil. Our zeal will be guided by knowledge and tempered with love for both God and man. Humility becomes the characteristic of our souls. It is the opposite of self-will toward God and ill will toward man. Discipline and suffering are effective schoolmasters that produce mildness in us, making the acceptance of instruction or admonition from the least of saints possible.

Once again let's consider how meekness fits in with the other Beatitudes. Being poor in spirit, we have had a full, piercing conviction of our utter sinfulness, guilt, and helplessness that casts us upon Christ. We are lost, undone, and stripped of all. Mourning weeps for our offenses against God and over the flesh in us that fails God. We then seek meekness (see Zeph. 2:3) for this to be changed in us. We fear our flesh and do not fight God's dealings with it. Then we hunger and thirst for the whole of righteousness that is outside of ourselves, not only to be imputed but also practically imparted to our walk. Mourning has softened the heart. Meekness makes us pliant, submissive and teachable. The meek become beautified with salvation (Ps. 149:4). The promise to inherit the earth is granted to the meek. This is a quote from Ps. 37:11, which deals with being envious of the prosperity of the wicked. The promise is also close to:

> *"The Spirit of the Lord God is upon Me, Because the Lord has anointed Me to preach **good tidings to the poor;**"* (Is. 61:1)

> *"Also your people shall all be righteous; **they shall inherit the land forever,** The branch of My planting, The work of My hands, That I may be glorified."* (Is. 60:21)

> *"Instead of your shame you shall have double honor, And instead of confusion they shall rejoice in their portion. **Therefore in their land they shall possess double;** Everlasting joy shall be theirs."* (Is. 61:7)

This promise is both present and future. Even now, as the meek possess their souls, they can possess what God has given them. They are pleased because God is pleased. Their joy is heaven, so they can enjoy earth without grasping at it. Regarding the future, those who are teachable now can be trusted with authority later. When we are delivered from a greedy, grasping disposition, we can enjoy what we have. This is part of the teaching of Psalm 37:11 - "But the meek shall inherit the earth," and "A little that a righteous man has is better than the riches of many wicked." (Ps. 37:16).

Proverbs agrees with this, stating that better is a little with the fear of the Lord than great pleasure with trouble (Pro. 15:16). Literally, we can enjoy all things now (see 1 Cor. 3:21-22; 2 Cor. 6:10). Also in the future, we have a better portion than the things of time. Such are the precious promises to the meek:

*"The poor shall eat and **be satisfied;**"* (Ps. 22:26)

*"The Lord **lifts up the humble;**"* (Ps. 147:6)

*"The humble also **shall increase their joy in the Lord**,"* (Is. 29:19)

All believers are to pursue meekness. It is to be shown unto all men (Titus 3:2). A meek and quiet spirit is of great price in the sight of the Lord (1 Pet. 3:4). It is especially important that meekness be present in our relationships to one another in the Body of Christ (Eph. 4:1-3; Col. 3:12). It is a necessary quality for leadership (1 Cor. 4:21; 1 Tim. 6:11). When we admonish one another, it is the meekness of Christ that has power. Authority in the church is not achieved by force; however, it is realized by one who possesses a servant's heart (Luke 22:24-27). People will submit when they know that they are loved and see meekness. It wins where violence fails (2 Tim. 2:24-26; Gal. 6:1). To restore one in the "spirit of meekness" means that the reinstatement is "not harsh, censorious, or out of a desire to discipline."

Thought Questions

1. Jesus gave an example of the fruit of meekness in Matthew 5:38-42. To which characteristics of meekness did He refer?

2. In God's orderly development of grace on the tables of our hearts, meekness is imparted after poverty of spirit and mourning. Why could meekness not precede the other two?

3. Discuss three situations in which the responses of Biblical personalities suggest "meekness is not weakness."

4. How can the promise that the meek will inherit the earth be both present and future?

5. Why do you think meekness is a necessary quality for those in leadership?

Chapter Twenty

"Blessed are those who hunger and thirst for righteousness, For they shall be filled. (Matt. 5:6)

Various scriptures use terms such as hungering and thirsting as metaphors for desiring spiritual things. There is water that springs up into everlasting life (John 4:13-14). The meat Jesus ate was doing the will of the Father (John 4:32-34). There is bread that endures to everlasting life (John 6:27). The Psalmist's tears were his food (Ps. 42:3). Job esteemed the words of God more than his necessary food (Job. 23:12). Isaiah invites us to buy wine and milk without money and without price (Is. 55:1).

The concept of hungering and thirsting after righteousness was different from the mindset of the religious thinkers of Jesus' day. The scribes and Pharisees considered righteousness as consisting of outward acts, such as almsgiving (Matt. 6:1). To this, the most special reward was promised. They taught a "works-righteousness" believing that almsgiving merited them the world to come and made them perfectly righteous. The rabbis taught that there were the perfectly righteous and the perfectly unrighteous; however, they certainly did not teach a concept of hungering and thirsting after righteousness.

Let us understand righteousness as Jesus taught it. It is in contrast to the teaching of the scribes and Pharisees. Righteousness is perhaps the main thrust of the Sermon on the Mount (Matt. 5:6,10,20; 6:1,33).

The righteousness of the scribes and Pharisees was completely external in nature. They obeyed the letter of the Law without any consideration for the spirit or purpose of the Law. Indeed, they had no comprehension of the love of God that motivated the Law. Quite often, they lifted the letter of the Law completely out of its context and used it to serve their own lusts!

The New Testament teaches that righteousness is first imputed (Rom. 4:3) and then imparted to do an inward and sanctifying work that is practically shown in our walk. These two aspects should never be separated. The one leads to the other. Salvation is receiving a new heart (Ezek. 36:26-27) and out of it springs the issues of life (Prov. 4:23; Matt. 12:34-35). Righteousness, then, is first and foremost holiness of heart and life, which then evidences itself through outward conduct. That which we have received by faith is worked into our walk. Consider righteousness as the working out of our salvation. A constant theme of Isaiah is that God's salvation brings practical righteousness:

> *"Rain down, you heavens, from above, **And let the skies pour down righteousness;** Let the earth open, **let them bring forth salvation,** And let righteousness spring up together. I, the Lord, have created it."* (Is. 45:8)

> *"Listen to Me, you stubborn-hearted, Who are far from righteousness: **I bring My righteousness near, it shall not be far off; My salvation shall not linger.** And I will place salvation in Zion, For Israel My glory."* (Is. 46:12,13)

"My righteousness is near; My salvation has gone forth, And My arms will judge the peoples; The coastlines will wait upon Me, And on My arm they will trust." (Is. 51:5)

"I will greatly rejoice in the Lord, My soul shall be joyful in my God; **For He has clothed me with the garments of salvation, He has covered me with the robes of righteousness,"** (Is. 61:10)

Now, let us consider the position of this Beatitude among the others. It is the first positive one; the first three deal with the removal of hindrances (negative aspects) from the human heart that work against true spirituality.

Recognizing poverty of spirit creates a sense of need and a realization of nothingness. It removes pride. Mourning causes us to judge self and gives us a consciousness of sorrow. It removes thoughtlessness and levity. Meekness causes an abandonment of pretenses and personal merit. It removes anger, impatience and discontent.

The fourth Beatitude turns the eye of the soul away from self to another. We are acutely conscious of the fact that we do not have righteousness, and we are fully aware that we urgently need it. It lies outside of ourselves; yet, we need it internalized. We have a fervent desire for the righteousness we do not possess. It is a yearning after Christ, who is the Lord our Righteousness (Jer. 23:6; 33:16).

The Holy Spirit has brought before our consciousness the holy and inexorable requirements of God. Our soul, being convicted of its destitution and guilt, realizes our lost condition and need of God's teaching. The Holy Spirit has created in us a deep hunger that causes us to seek relief from Christ, the Lord our Righteousness.

Man was created to be a vessel for the life of God. God made man upright (Eccl. 7:29). However, when Adam sinned, man became filled with himself, rather than filled with God. This created the false appetites of the flesh, causing man to short-circuit his potential. The first three Beatitudes are the undoing of those fleshly appetites. Their removal causes the true appetite of the inner man to return. Hunger and thirst are strong appetites, and once awakened, the spiritual appetite swallows up all else. A strong yearning to be renewed after the image of Him who created us fills the heart (Col. 3:10). Rightness in relationship was lacking, but it is now longed for (2 Cor. 3:18; Rom. 1:17).

The metaphor of hunger and thirst would have made a strong impression on those listening to Jesus preach. A workingman would only eat meat once a week. The hot winds and sandstorms would cause suffocation, creating intense thirst unknown to western culture. Unless we eat and drink, we perish! The question is: How strongly do we desire goodness? Is our desire sharp and passionate? Do we long for righteousness with our whole heart?

There are two important lessons not observable to the English reader that the Greek text would teach us. The words "hunger" and "thirst" in normal Greek usage are always followed by the word "of." For instance, a translation into English would be "I hunger for of bread." This rightly implies that you desire some bread, but not the whole loaf. However, in the verse before us (Matt. 5:6), the word "of" is not there, and this is an exception to the normal Greek grammar. Jesus is teaching us that we are to hunger and thirst after the whole of righteousness, complete righteousness, before God and man - not just a portion of it. We want our entire conduct to flow out of a righteousness inscribed upon the tables of our hearts. It is to be in all areas of our lives, not just some parts. A man may be morally honest and highly respected, but he can't listen to a sad story or offer a sympathetic ear to someone in need. On the other hand, a drunkard may be very compassionate to those in need and very freely give assistance to them! Neither case reflects the whole righteousness of Christ.

Secondly, the Greek translation has the article "the" before the word righteousness. This definitely implies that there is only one righteousness related to God. Indeed, the human soul can never be satisfied unless it contains the whole righteousness of God. The first three Beatitudes have convinced us that righteousness lies outside ourselves and God Himself must engrave it on the tables of our hearts.

We should always note that the hungering and thirsting are both initial and continuous experiences. Having been set free from the penalty of sin, we yearn to be set free from the very presence of sin. This is a continuous experience, only to be relieved at the future appearing of Christ when we shall be glorified with Him! In that day, all creation will be released from its groaning into the glorious liberty of the sons of God (Rom. 8:19-25)! Until then, like Paul, "we groan, earnestly desiring to be clothed with our habitation which is from heaven." (2 Cor. 5:1-5).

This craving is continuous until that perfect day. It is a longing for full salvation, when the very presence of sin is removed from all of God's creation (2 Pet. 3:13). Meanwhile, we long for a greater and more perfect conformity to the image of Christ (Rom. 8:29). As the Psalmist, our souls thirst for God (Ps. 42:1-2). Being renewed in the image of Christ, our soul aspires for the divine blessings that alone can strengthen, sustain, and satisfy it.

Outward observances and religion cannot satisfy. Paul discovered the truth of this fact and discusses the life-changing influence it had upon him in Phil. 3:4-15. These can neither replace the knowledge of God in Christ Jesus nor impart the life that is hidden with Christ in God. They will not join us to the

Lord in one spirit or grant fellowship with the Father and Son. Only when righteousness revealed from heaven is inscribed on the tables of our hearts will we know what it is to walk in the light of God and to be pure as He is pure. It will cause us to go within the veil and to be at rest in God. Being seated in heavenly places will not be a theory; it will be a divine reality of the soul. Righteousness revealed from heaven and written on our hearts will cause us to be filled with a peace that passes all understanding, overflowing with the goodness and mercy of God, and abounding in praise and thanksgiving. This craving for the righteousness of God cries out, "Let me not live but to be holy as You are holy!"

The promise is that those who hunger and thirst will be filled. The statement emphatically declares that only those who hunger and thirst after righteousness will be filled. This lies close to terminology used when speaking of the Holy Spirit. The New Testament record is that they were "filled" with the Holy Spirit. Perhaps the reason why some are not gloriously "filled" is because they are not first "emptied." We try to experience the fourth Beatitude without the preparation of the first three. The New Testament church was full because it was empty! The promise is sure!

Notice that the promise is not to those who have attained but to those who crave. On this earth, there will always be a need for a greater conformity to Christ! But now, for those who hunger and thirst, they shall be filled. We shall rest with God in this life, which is a foretaste of that which is eternal in nature! Having the hope that we shall be like Him, we purify ourselves now (1 John 3:2-3). In that day, when we behold His face in righteousness and awaken in His likeness, we shall be at long last fully satisfied (Ps. 17:15). On that day, there shall be hunger and thirst no more (Rev. 7:16)!

Thought Questions

1. Contrast the concepts of righteousness as expressed by the scribes and Pharisees and by Jesus.

2. If you were asked to summarize Paul's discussion in Philippians 3:4-15, what would you say to substantiate his theme "Outward observances and religion cannot satisfy?"

3. Describe the intensity of the hungering and thirsting that births the promise "they shall be filled." With what shall they be filled?

4. When will the believer no longer hunger and thirst after righteousness? When will those cravings be fully complete? Why will they be satisfied then?

5. Discuss the need to be 'emptied' before one can be 'filled.'

Blessed Are Those Who Hunger and Thirst for Righteousness

Chapter Twenty-One

> Pureness of heart does not mean sinless perfection; but rather, it means that the heart possesses not only a sincere desire not to sin against God in thought, word or deed but also a resolution to please Him in all things. A pure heart is conscious of the dangers of fleshly desires and sets up a standard against their intrusion into a believer's life.

**"Blessed are the merciful,
For they shall obtain mercy."
(Matt. 5:7)**

As with the other Beatitudes, this one must be considered in the order in which it appears. Jesus is contrasting the effects of the Law engraved upon the heart with the self-righteous interpretation of the scribes and Pharisees. He is describing for us the true characteristics of those who are subject to the kingdom of heaven, those who are truly blessed.

The first four beatitudes describe the initial exercises of the heart as the law penetrates it. The first three remove the negative forces of self, while the fourth unveils the God-given appetites of the inner man. The next four Beatitudes are subsequent fruits, of which mercy is the first evidence of being filled with righteousness. Once God has uncovered our state, we know we are in no position to judge others. We know that God has dealt mercifully and graciously with us. Having come to know ourselves and to recognize that we have been pardoned, how could we possibly pass judgment on others?

The fruit of this process is God's nature reproduced in us by writing His laws inwardly on our hearts. The great revelation of the nature of God is His mercy. When Moses asked for a glimpse of God's glory, he received a mighty revelation of the mercy of God (Ex. 34:6-7):

> *"And the Lord passed before him and proclaimed, 'The Lord, the Lord God, **merciful** and gracious, longsuffering, and abounding in goodness and truth, keeping **mercy for thousands**, forgiving iniquity and transgression and sin,' "*

The goals of God are always guided by His mercy. As James said:

> *"Indeed we count them blessed who endure. You have heard of the perseverance of Job and seen the end intended by the Lord – that the Lord is very compassionate and **merciful**."* (James 5:11)

Having received grace, how can we be anything but gracious toward others? The truth is that our relationship with God is only as real as the genuineness of our dealings with others in righteousness and mercy.

The Ten Commandments teach us how to love God and neighbor. So do the Beatitudes. The first four Beatitudes relate us to God. Now, this one tells us to love our neighbor by showing him mercy.

Mercy is something we learn as a result of God working in us. It describes something we become, not just something we do. It develops into an operative principle within the springs of our hearts. Mercy is not a negative quality in the sense that we don't deal harshly with others, but it is a positive value since we pro-

214

ceed from an active kindness. Matthew's use of the word (Matt. 9:27; 15:22; 17:15) shows that the emphasis is on pity demonstrated by action and not just on thought.

The word "mercy" is difficult to translate from the Greek (eleemon) or Hebrew (chesedh). An attempt would be to describe mercy as the outward manifestation of pity shown in active kindness. It assumes the need on the part of him who receives it and adequate resources on the part of him who shows it. Mercy is a holy compassion of soul that moves us to pity. Seeing misery in another, we are stirred to action. Mercy makes the case of another its own, as if it was the one in misery. Hearts are touched and stirred within. It is a spirit of kindness and benevolence. It tempers justice with mercy and scorns revenge. It weeps with those who weep, as one with them. It is compassion that God approves, a fruit of the Spirit, and the manifestation of Christ in us.

Mercy is not just an emotional wave of pity, nor a foolish sentimentality that ignores sin and the requirements of justice; rather, it is a sympathy that comes from a deliberate identification. It is to get under another person's skin, to see with his eyes, to think with his thoughts, and to feel with his feelings. Mercy then takes another's case as its own and actively seeks to relieve the misery. It prefers alleviating the cause and giving space for repentance to issuing judgment. Mercy triumphs over judgment (James 2:13). Is this not what God did with us in Christ Jesus?

> *"Therefore, in all things He had to be made like His brethren, that He might be **a merciful and faithful High Priest in things pertaining to God**, to make propitiation for the sins of the people."* (Heb. 2:17)

When mercy is part of our nature, we find offering forgiveness and tolerance much easier. However, we must learn not to be kind in the wrong way. Martha was trying to be kind to Jesus, but He neither wanted nor required a big meal (Luke 10:38-42). He wanted quiet and close relationship before He went to Jerusalem to be crucified! Mercy takes into account the needs of the one being loved.

Being filled with the righteousness of God, we naturally show mercy (Ps. 37:21). It is evidence of God's love in us (1 John 3:17). Mercy is something we are commanded to provide with cheerfulness (Rom. 12:8). Abraham, though wronged by Lot, demonstrated mercy when he rescued his nephew. Joseph exemplified it when he forgave his brothers. Moses prayed for Miriam's healing, and David spared Saul. Lack of mercy is part of an evil man's downfall (Ps. 109:16).

To the merciful, God shows Himself merciful. This is the promise. The one who shows mercy is doubly blessed. Firstly, there is an inward satisfaction in showing mercy. The merciful man does good to his own soul (Prov. 11:17). He that shows mercy to the poor is happy (Prov. 14:21). Secondly, it determines how God deals with us, both now and at the judgment to come. This principle is made abundantly clear throughout the scripture. He that follows after righteousness and mercy finds life, righteousness, and honor (Prov. 21:21). God deals with us in the same manner we deal with others: uprightly with the upright, purely with the pure, and deviously with the devious (Ps. 18:25-26). Thus, we are not to judge, lest we be judged (Matt. 7:1).

This principle of reaping what we sow can be found throughout scripture. Forgiveness comes as we forgive others (Matt. 6:12; 14-15; 18:35). At the judgment, we will be treated as we have treated others (Matt. 25:31-46). Did not Sodom and Gomorrah suffer fire and brimstone in response to their burning lusts? Pharaoh, who ordered the drowning of infants, had his own army drowned at the Red Sea while in pursuit of the children of

Israel. Jacob's sons tricked him concerning the fate of Joseph; however, Jacob had deceived his father Isaac by pretending to be Esau.

Nadab and Abihu, the sons of Aaron offered strange fire and were consumed by fire. David, after committing adultery with Bathsheba and arranging the murder of her husband Uriah, had his sons commit adultery within his own family; and vengeance was carried out by strong drink and murder. The Lord is aware of every little detail, His eyes beholding good and evil in every place (Prov. 15:3).

This principle is observable not only concerning evil, but also regarding good. Those who give shall receive (2 Cor. 9:6). The Lord will recompense any man for whatever good thing he does (Eph. 6:8). Those who show mercy now will be treated mercifully at the judgment to come (James 2:13; 2 Tim. 1:12,16-18). As we show mercy to others, so God deals mercifully with us, understanding us, and alleviating our sufferings.

Mercy is to be found in our interpersonal relationships. When Paul wrote to a body of believers, his usual greeting included grace and peace. However, when writing to an individual, he may add the word "mercy" (1 Tim. 1:2; 2 Tim. 1:2; Titus 1:4).

Thought Questions

1. When Moses asked God for a glimpse of His glory, what did He give him?

2. James states that mercy triumphs over judgment (James 2:13). How do you interpret this statement in the light of Hebrews 2:17?

3. The principle of reaping what we sow is frequently illustrated in Scripture. What are some examples of this principle that are not provided in this text?

4. *"The merciful man does good for his own soul, But he who is cruel troubles his own flesh." (Prov. 11:17).* Certainly King Solomon knew the truth of this proverb in his own life. How do you expect its truth to influence you as you allow the Spirit to write it on your heart?

5. Describe how a person behaves towards others when mercy is fully manifest in that person's character.

Chapter Twenty-Two

> Pureness of heart does not mean
> sinless perfection; but rather, it
> means that the heart possesses not
> only a sincere desire not to sin
> against God in thought, word or
> deed but also a resolution to
> please Him in all things.

"Blessed are the pure in heart,
For they shall see God."
(Matt. 5:8)

As with the other Beatitudes, we are tracing the work of God in the heart as the Spirit of God writes His law on it. The result is that we become empty of self and filled with His righteousness. The first four Beatitudes have purified our hearts, eliminating those things in us that are contrary to establishing and maintaining communion with Him. For two to walk together, they must be agreed (Amos 3:3).

The second four Beatitudes are evidences or subsequent fruit of that working. First, we are merciful to others, even as God has been merciful to us. This is evidence before man. The present Beatitude, being pure in heart, is evidence before God. Therefore, the blessing of those who keep their hearts pure is that they see God, even as Adam did in the beginning. Sin no longer clouds their vision of God. A clean heart is necessary:

> *"But your **iniquities have separated you from your God;
> and your sins have hidden His face from you**, So that
> He will not hear."* (Is. 59:2)

It should be remembered that Jesus is exposing the error of the scribes and Pharisees, whose righteousness was totally external. Their "purity" was only "legal" in the sense of Levitical distinctions of clean and unclean. They failed to realize that the heart is the source of all the issues of life (Prov. 4:23). It is the seat of the affections and understanding. The heart is the source that governs our speech and actions (Matt. 12:34-35).

King David understood this. Therefore, after he sinned, he asked for cleansing in his heart (Ps. 51:6,10). It is plain that the scribes and Pharisees missed this simple point. Many stories in Matthew's gospel illustrate that indeed was the case (c.f. Matt. 15:11-20). However, even Moses the lawgiver understood this. He spoke a prophetic word lamenting the fact that God's people do not have the heart to keep His commandments (Deut. 5:29). The law is to lead to a pure heart (1 Tim. 1:5) and we are to love the Lord with all our heart (Deut. 6:5). The New Testament insists that we live and serve from the heart (Eph. 6:6). This, the majority of the religious leaders of Jesus' day did not own (c.f. Matt. 5:28,37). The New Testament is a religion of the heart:

> *"I will give you a **new heart and put a new spirit within you; I will take the heart of stone out of your flesh and give you a heart of flesh.** I will put My Spirit within you and cause you to walk in My statutes, and you will keep My judgments and do them."* (Ezek. 36:26-27)

> *"But the Lord said to Samuel, 'Do not look at his appearance or at his physical stature, because I have refused him. For the Lord does not see as a man sees; for man looks at the outward appearance, **but the Lord looks at the heart.**'"* (1 Sam. 16:7)

The Psalmist makes it clear that a pure heart is a prerequisite for drawing near to God. A pure heart is necessary to ascend into the hill of the Lord, to stand in His holy place (Ps. 24:3-4). Truly, God is good to such as are of a clean heart (Ps. 73:1).

This Beatitude also refers to a condition that must be maintained. We are to call on the Lord out of a pure heart (2 Tim. 2:22). We are to love with a pure heart fervently (1 Pet. 1:22). The work of the Holy Spirit is to purify the heart (Acts 15:8-9).

A pure heart is a heart that has been cleansed from pollutions. The Greek word for pure is "katharos" and is used in the following manners. **Firstly**, it means clean as in washed clothes. **Secondly**, it is used to describe grain that has been winnowed or sifted. It means the chaff has been removed. **Thirdly**, it is used of a purged army that has dismissed its ineffective, unwilling, discontented soldiers, so that what is left is a first-class group of fighting men. **Fourthly**, it means to be unmixed or unadulterated. Therefore, a pure heart is one that has been cleansed from impurities. There are no mixed motives, but it only seeks to glorify God. Only the heart united can continuously fear His name, praise Him, and glorify His name forevermore:

Teach me Your way, O Lord; I will walk in Your truth; **Unite my heart to fear Your name. I will praise You, O Lord my God, with all my heart**, *And I will glorify Your name forevermore.* " (Ps. 86:11-12)

Pureness of heart does not mean sinless perfection; but rather, it means that the heart possesses not only a sincere desire not to sin against God in thought, word or deed but also a resolution to please Him in all things. A pure heart is conscious of the dangers of fleshly desires and sets up a standard against their intrusion into a believer's life. Love for God is not shared with anything else (c.f. Luke 14:26-27). Since there is no desire for recognition or prestige, God receives the praise, honor, and glory.

We were created for fellowship with God. The state of the heart is obviously an enormous factor in this. Christ is to "make Himself at home in our hearts" (Eph. 3:14-19). Self and sin blind the heart, while purity enables it to see. The faith that purifies the heart prepares the heart to see God in life and to enjoy a more extensive and intimate fellowship with Him. Think of the heart as a window through which God shines into us. A dirty window lets in less light and obscures our vision as well. A pure heart enjoys the vision of God. It is as if God says, "Be like Me and you will see Me!" (See 1 John 3:2-3).

The pure in heart see God. This implies to be brought near to Him, to enjoy Him, and to have spiritual sight and discernment. One whose heart has been made pure by embracing the first four Beatitudes will recognize the hand of God in all things: in creation, in His providence, and in His dealings. A pure heart is enabled to see and appreciate what could not be discerned before. We learn not to see circumstances but to see God! We see what we are trained to see. An astronomer will see shape, beauty, and many minute details as he gazes into the heavens at night. His eyes take in so much more than those of the uninitiated. A botanist beholds innumerable untold wonders as he looks over a marsh. Even so, the pure in heart has been trained and educated and can see with clearer vision the hand and wonders of God that were so obscure before.

Not only is this a present promise but also assurance of a fuller vision to come. Now we see through a mirror dimly (1 Cor. 13:12), but then face to face. We will see Him as He is; those filled with this hope will purify themselves (1 John 3:2-3). The day shall come when we shall see His face (Rev. 22:4). For this reason, we are to endeavor to keep our hearts clean. Isaiah tells us to correct our conduct (Is. 1:16). Paul admonishes us to cleanse ourselves from all filthiness of the flesh and spirit (2 Cor. 7:1). Peter instructs us to sanctify the Lord God in our hearts (1 Pet. 3:15). The Psalmist set the Lord always before him (Ps. 16:8), and David cries out for a clean heart, for truth in the inward parts (Ps. 51:6,10,17).

Though having the hardness of the heart ploughed up may seem difficult, the vision of God to be received at the end brings untold peace into an otherwise tumultuous world.

Thought Questions

1. Why is a pure heart necessary in approaching God?

2. What are the four definitions of the word "pure?"

3. How do the pure in heart "see" God?

4. Does the promise to see God have both a present and future application? Explain.

5. What does this Beatitude mean to you personally?

Chapter Twenty-Three

By learning righteousness, we enter the kingdom of heaven now and prepare for the kingdom's full and final consummation and glory yet to be revealed. For all eternity, we are glorious members and partakers of the kingdom of heaven! Hallelujah!

**"Blessed are the peacemakers,
For they shall be called sons of God."
(Matt. 5:9)**

To the warlike Galileans, thoughts of peace would be distasteful. They would rather conquer all nations than make peace.

Let us inquire into the meaning of the word "peace." The Hebrew word is "shalom" and the Greek word is "eirene." It not only means the absence of trouble or evil things but also includes everything that makes for a man's highest good. To wish peace to someone is to ask for the presence of good things and to seek every blessing relating to spirit, soul, and body in time and eternity (1 Thess. 5:23). All of Paul's epistles begin with a salutation of grace and peace. On behalf of his readers, Paul requests peace that brings enjoyment of all God's blessings, both spiritual and temporal.

Let us recognize what peace is not. Peace is not failure to deal with issues that may be explosive. It is not a failure to confront what may be an undercurrent that brings a sense of nervousness to any situation. Peace is never achieved at the expense of truth, righteousness, or holiness (Matt. 10:34; Heb. 12:14). Notice the order of the Beatitudes. Peace follows purity! The wisdom from above is first pure before it is peaceable (James 3:17). Avoidance of issues in the name of keeping peace only serves to create a nervous tension that is anything but peaceful. Failure to confront allows a dangerous situation to develop.

Just as the phrase "pure in heart" modifies the "merciful" preceding it, it also qualifies the "peacemakers" following it. Inward holiness manifests itself in outward conduct.

Notice that the promise of the seventh Beatitude is not for "peacelovers" but for "peacemakers." It refers to more than a peaceable person, one who avoids conflicts. We are told to be at peace with one another (Mark 9:50) and as much as possible, live peaceably with all men (Rom. 12:18). A peacemaker has a peaceable character that consciously exerts itself outwardly. It is a dynamic grace. God actively made peace through the blood of the cross (Col. 1:20). Peacemakers are lovers of God and man; they abhor strife and contention and prevent their being kindled or spread further if started. Peacemakers preserve and restore peace, taking joy in promoting goodwill. They do good to all men. The preaching of the gospel is the spreading of the message of peace (Rom. 10:15). Peacemakers seek to establish right relationships among men. Bitterness cannot exist with them. They build bridges, heal breaches, and sweeten bitterness: they seek to promote the opposite of division.

As with the other Beatitudes, note its place in their order. This is the first Beatitude that states a blessing upon a person doing a "work" (peacemaking); the previous ones refer to a "quality" in them (poor in spirit, meek, merciful). Peacemaking is the summation of all the other Beatitudes and qualities. Ephesians 4:1-3 states the same thing. It takes a meek, merciful and forbearing individual to be a peacemaker.

Being a peacemaker takes wisdom, courage, tact, and love. Often a peacemaker may be regarded as an enemy to both sides of a dispute! Romans 12:18 implies that this may be a difficult task at times. Nevertheless, the peacemaker acts because he has entered into peace himself and seeks to promote the best interest of all. The work done in his own heart evidences itself spontaneously. He loves peace from the heart and diligently seeks it with all men. The warring elements in his soul have been subdued.

God's nature is being reproduced in us. Many times God is referred to as the God of peace (Rom. 15:33; 2 Cor. 13:11; 1 Thess. 5:23; Heb. 13:20; Phil. 4:9). God is a peacemaker. That is the nature of God and His sons! God's sons love peace, as God loves it.

The word "children" in the King James Version is actually "sons" which means full grown, developed, mature sons. Because they have God's character fully developed in them, these sons of God love peace from the heart and move to promote it when they can. They exhibit proof that they are the sons of God. This is what John the Baptist demanded (Matt. 3:8).

The Hebrew language does not tend to use adjectives as the English language does. To describe a person, the appropriate noun would be placed at the end of a phrase. A good example of this is found in Acts 4:36; there, Barnabas is called a Son of Encouragement. Encouragement is the noun that describes the quality found in Barnabas. Jesus says that peacemakers are called sons of God (Matt. 5:9). Therefore, God is the noun that describes the qualities found in peacekeepers. Consider the multitude of admirable attributes that make up God's nature. Stand in awe of the God who transforms men into His image so that He can call them peacekeepers, sons of God!

The significance of the term "sons of God" includes both the nature of sonship and the privilege of sonship. Peacemakers are prepared for adoption as the sons of God (Rom. 8:14-23). Having taken on the nature of Christ, the Prince of Peace (Is. 9:6), they can be entrusted to share in His inheritance.

God recognizes them as His sons who take on His work of reconciliation as their own. Many times peacemakers give up earthly privileges in order to bring peace to others. To be called peacemakers by God is to be honored by God: God takes pleasure in such an announcement.

Thought Questions

1. *"Do not think that I came to bring peace on earth. I did not come to bring peace but a sword."* Jesus is a peacemaker; however, His statement in Matthew 10:34 appears to negate this fact. Explain.

2. "Peacemakers seek to establish right relationships among men." Have you been actively engaged in bringing peace to family, church, and community situations where strife was destroying peaceful living? Describe your influential involvement.

3. "The significance of the term 'sons of God' includes both the nature of sonship and the privilege of sonship." Comment on this statement.

4. Is there a difference between a "peacelover" and a "peacemaker?" Explain.

5. Why do you think this Beatitude is the seventh in the list? How is it placed in relation to the other Beatitudes in order of their development?

Blessed Are the Peacemakers

Chapter Twenty-Four

The Beatitudes undo the self and sin by which the world is governed, thereby exposing it. The Christian lifestyle acts as a conscience to society, and consequently it is attacked, criticized, and ridiculed.

"Blessed are those who are persecuted for righteousness' sake, For theirs is the kingdom of heaven.

Blessed are you when they revile and persecute you, and say all kinds of evil against you falsely for My sake. Rejoice and be exceedingly glad, for great is your reward in heaven, for so they persecuted the prophets who were before you." (Matt. 5:10-12)

Notice that the reward for the last Beatitude is the same as for the first one. The Beatitudes therefore describe the practical righteousness that is descriptive of those who experientially enter the kingdom of heaven. It is the effect of the Law of God being engraved on the tables of our hearts. Notice, too, that the last Beatitude in the first group deals with hungering and thirsting after righteousness and that the last of the second group of four speaks of being persecuted for righteousness' sake. The kingdom of heaven issues forth in righteousness.

As Matthew uses the term, the kingdom of heaven takes on three discernable shades of meaning. **Firstly**, in Matthew 13, Jesus uses the phrase in parables to describe all who profess belief in Christ, both true and false. **Secondly**, as in the Sermon on the Mount and throughout the gospel, the kingdom of heaven describes a spiritual reality now, a righteousness formed in our character as God progressively deals with us. **Thirdly**, it carries forward the idea that the full manifestation of the kingdom of heaven is yet to come, being fully revealed at the return of Christ. Then there will be a reward proportionate to the degree we have learned righteousness now.

The righteous character that is formed in us is opposite to the spirit of the world. The Beatitudes undo the self and sin by which the world is governed, thereby exposing it. The Christian lifestyle acts as a conscience to society, and consequently it is attacked, criticized, and ridiculed. Lack of tolerance for the Christian by the world is the greatest proof that he is not of it.

Matthew's definition of righteousness needs to be understood, as this is the cause of persecution. Righteousness is one of the great themes of his gospel. His purpose in writing was to counteract wrong concepts of the Law, especially as held by the scribes and Pharisees. Some relax the commandments of God (Matt. 5:19) and teach others to do so. To say that righteousness does not matter for Christians in an age of grace is a perversion of grace, and in Matthew's estimation, it is the root cause of the church's ills! Grace is the righteousness of the Law revealed in us and is operative as a life principle in us. This is not different from the apostle Paul's view (Rom. 8:4; Gal. 5:23). The Spirit of God writes the Laws of God on our hearts; thus, they become the life principle working itself out by the force of its own motions.

To Matthew, right living is the end of the gospel. Righteousness is mentioned twenty-five times in twenty-eight chapters! Jesus is portrayed as walking in the righteousness of God. His first words recorded by Matthew declared that He came to fulfill all righteousness (Matt. 3:15). To Matthew, righteousness is doing right in the eyes of the Lord. It is rightness of heart and rightness of conduct. Matthew derives his understanding of righteousness from the prophets, from passages such as Ezek. 18:5-9, and gives it the meaning of doing justly. Such conduct is obviously opposite to that of the world; consequently, it invites the world's antagonism. Jesus states that such would be the case. Paul states it; Peter especially exhorts along these lines:

*"If the world hates you, **you know that it hated Me before it hated you.**"* (John 15:18)

*"They will put you out of the synagogues; yes, the time is coming that **whoever kills you will think that he offers God service.**"* (John 16:2)

*"Yes, and all who desire to live godly lives in Christ Jesus **will suffer persecution.**"* (2 Tim. 3:12)

*"Beloved, do not think it strange concerning the fiery trial which is to try you, as though some strange thing happened to you; but rejoice to the extent that you partake of Christ's sufferings, that when His glory is revealed, you may also be glad with exceeding joy. **If you are reproached for the name of Christ, blessed are you, for the Spirit of glory and of God rests upon you.** On their part He is blasphemed, but on your part He is glorified."* (1 Pet. 4:12-14)

Consider the persecution of the early believers. What a cost they paid for righteousness' sake! They lost employment; they wouldn't do business contracts to build heathen temples; they went without rather than compromise truth. Their social lives were touched. Many of the common meals often started with a drink offering to a heathen god. Of course, they could not partake of that offering. Family members disowned them. Christians were objects of slander, continuously. The heathens charged them with cannibalism when they partook of the Lord's Supper. Charges of immorality surrounded their love feasts. Their stand on end times caused them to appear as revolutionaries. They were blamed for the division of families. Their refusal to worship Caesar made them enemies of Rome. Caesar-worship was the unifying factor of the Roman Empire. All were required to offer a pinch of incense and say that Caesar is lord. Then one would be free to worship other gods. The Christians would not do this; consequently, they became the objects of severe persecution.

Who were the ones being persecuted, and by whom were they persecuted? Those who were born after the flesh persecuted those who were born after the Spirit (Gal. 4:29). The righteous are persecuted by an evil world (1 John 3:12-13). The ungodly persecute those who live godly (2 Tim. 3:12). In Matthew's gospel, the persecution came from the "religious" leaders who opposed Christ and His teachings.

Persecution is to be worn as a badge of honor by the Christian, for it is to be considered a privilege (Phil. 1:28-29). It is the world's testimony that we are not of it, and it is God's testimony that we are fit to serve Him. It is proof that God considers us ready for promotion, for tests only come to those who are able to pass them! It is God's statement that we are qualified for something greater. This is exactly the attitude the early church took in the face of persecution. They rejoiced that they were counted worthy to suffer for His name (Acts 5:41). They would sing praises at midnight in jail (Acts 16:25). They realized that if they endured, they would also reign (2 Tim. 2:12). Indeed, the sufferings of this present world are not worthy to be compared with the glory that shall be revealed in us (Rom. 8:18)!

In this Beatitude, Jesus changes from saying, "Blessed are they" to "Blessed are you." Also, in contrast to Matthew 5:6, there is no article in front of the word "righteousness." In other words, persecution comes for even displaying a "part" of righteousness.

As Christ was reviled at the hands of the scribes and Pharisees, so Christians will be despised. This means to suffer reproach, to suffer abuse. Being persecuted, believers will be harassed, hunted, and spoiled like a wild beast pursued by the hunter. Abuse is the lot of the believer from the unrighteous. Paul felt himself defamed by those who considered him the filth of the world and the offscouring of all things (1 Cor. 4:13). At Philippi, he had been shamefully entreated (1 Thess. 2:2). All manner of evil will be spoken against the believer in Christ. This is done falsely, not for wrong causes, but for right doing (1 Pet. 4:15-16). All this happens because of the work of Christ in our hearts: it is for His sake, for fidelity to His gospel.

Jesus tells us to rejoice when this happens! We are to rejoice and be exceeding glad! The only other time this phrase is used in scripture is the celebration over the defeat of the great whore in the book of Revelation (Rev. 19:7). It is an occasion for joy as the emotions are stirred. Why? The answer - God is preparing us for something far greater. We will be recompensed for what is lost in this world, and it will be a great reward. We are in good company. The prophets before us were persecuted in this manner as well.

The Beatitudes grant a satisfying life now, and they prepare us for the glory that shall be revealed. By learning righteousness, we enter the kingdom of heaven now and prepare for the kingdom's full and final consummation and glory yet to be revealed. For all eternity, we are glorious members and partakers of the kingdom of heaven!

Thought Questions

1. "The term 'kingdom of heaven' has three discernable shades of meaning. Briefly discuss each of these nuances.

2. What is Matthew's understanding of the word "righteousness?"

3. "Persecution is to be worn as a badge of honor by the Christian." Discuss this statement in the light of Paul's comments in Philippians 1:28-29.

4. Why does the world persecute the Christian?

5. What kind of suffering did the original readers of the New Testament experience? Is it paralleled today?

6. What is the proper biblical reaction to suffering for righteousness' sake?

References

Caffin, B.C., Adeney, W.F., Barker, P.C., Dods, Marcus, MacDonald, J.A., Tuck, R.. (1892) The Pulpit Commentary (Vol. 15), Wm. B. Eerdmans Publishing Company, Grand Rapids, Michigan

Edersheim, Alfred, (1886) The Life and Times of Jesus the Messiah, Hendrickson Publishers, Peabody, Massachusetts.

Fee, Gordon & Stuart, Douglas (1993) How to Read the Bible for All Its Worth, Scripture Union, Bletchley, U.K.

Nee, Watchman (1978) The King and the Kingdom of Heaven, Christian Fellowship Publishers, Inc., New York

White, R. E. O., (1979) The Mind of Matthew, The Westminster Press, Philadelphia, Pennsylvania